ALL THAT GLITTERS

ALL THAT GLITTERS

A Climber's Journey

through Addiction

and Depression

MARGO TALBOT

RMB

For information on purchasing bulk quantities of this book, or to obtain media excerpts or invite
the author to speak at an event, please visit rmbooks.com and select the "Contact" tab.

RMB | Rocky Mountain Books Ltd.
rmbooks.com
@rmbooks
facebook.com/rmbooks

Cataloguing data available from Library and Archives Canada
ISBN 9781771604338 (paperback)
ISBN 9781771604345 (electronic)

All photographs are by the author unless otherwise noted.

Cover photo by Paul Zizka

Printed and bound in Canada

We would like to also take this opportunity to acknowledge the traditional territories upon which
we live and work. In Calgary, Alberta, we acknowledge the Niitsítapi (Blackfoot) and the people of
the Treaty 7 region in Southern Alberta, which includes the Siksika, the Piikuni, the Kainai, the
Tsuut'ina and the Stoney Nakoda First Nations, including Chiniki, Bearpaw, and Wesley First Nations. The City of Calgary is also home to Métis Nation of Alberta, Region III. In Victoria, British
Columbia, we acknowledge the traditional territories of the Lkwungen (Esquimalt, and Songhees),
Malahat, Pacheedaht, Scia'new, T'Sou-ke and W̱SÁNEĆ (Pauquachin, Tsartlip, Tsawout, Tsey-
cum) peoples.

We acknowledge the financial support of the Government of Canada through the Canada Book
Fund and the Canada Council for the Arts, and of the province of British Columbia through the
British Columbia Arts Council and the Book Publishing Tax Credit.

To my parents, Frank and Sheila,
for giving me the gift of life, and for doing the best they
could given the resources they had.

To Karen McNeill,
for seeing the good in me before I saw it in myself,
and for helping me realize that my life was worth living.

To Warren Macdonald,
for showing me that I had wings, and could fly.

CONTENTS

FOREWORD

THE ALCHEMY OF GRIEF

ALTHOUGH I KNEW the broad contours of Margo's story – the troubled childhood, the bouts with addiction and depression, the redemption through climbing and community – I didn't fully appreciate her book prior to my own experience with indelible grief. Yet the cause of an individual's suffering need not be as dramatic and obvious as the abuse and addiction Margo depicts. Smaller disappointments and slights too can leave us reeling. Perhaps therein lies the value of Margo's words, for they reveal certain truths universal to our varied experiences as imperfect human beings facing an uncertain world.

Each of us travels a unique path punctuated by joy and sorrow, triumphs and setbacks both large and small. We gravitate toward joy, as we must. We seek the warmth of a loving partner, the comfort of family and friends. We celebrate our successes at work. We delight in those magical moments in the mountains or wherever we play. But we are conditioned to avoid the sorrows. Pain is seen as failure, an unnecessary step backwards. Suffering is to be avoided, shunted off to some dark corner where we hope it will stay. It seldom does.

Who among us hasn't lost a spouse, a parent, a close friend? Who hasn't been disappointed in love, or devastated by a life-altering illness? If we haven't thus far, we likely will, and sooner than we'd prefer. Someone within our circle almost certainly tolerates a loveless marriage, agonizes over an ailing parent, regrets a lost opportunity. *How are you doing?* We ask, though we don't really want to know the answer. We shy away from acknowledging each other's struggles, from offering a sympathetic shoulder on which to rest. We hope to inoculate ourselves. *There but for the grace of God go I.* Yet when we turn away, we not only dismiss that which makes us uncomfortable, we deny our own suffering and allow it an unseen power over our lives.

With a direct and brutal honesty, Margo peers deeply into her dark corners and takes us along on her journey to peace and enlightenment. She reminds us that the path is seldom straight and never easy. She knowingly engages in self-destructive behaviour, yet time and time again resurfaces and recommits herself to healing. She never gives up: she takes two steps forward and three back. She does the work. Eventually she falls "...into the abyss that had been waiting for me all my life." From this nadir she rekindles hope and climbs back toward the light.

As we all inevitably must. In October 2017, my wife Julie and I found out that our only son, Hayden, and the love of his life, Inge Perkins, had been caught in an avalanche in Montana. Both were buried. Hayden dug himself out and searched for Inge, to no avail. He took his life a few hours later, disconsolate and alone. Since then I've felt unmoored from the world. It is still incomprehensible to me that Hayden's life, so full of love and promise, is over, and I wonder when, if ever, the weight on my soul will lessen.

Margo's words give me hope as I navigate this river of grief. She provides a guidebook to the wilderness of desperation. More than anything, *All That Glitters* helps me understand how essential are these periods of sadness, these disappointments, these times fraught with angst and uncertainty, for it is on the forge of grief that we transmute suffering into joy.

—MICHAEL KENNEDY, OCTOBER 2019

PREFACE TO THE NEW EDITION

WHEN THIS BOOK WAS ORIGINALLY RELEASED in the spring of 2011, the Arab uprising was in full swing, the hunt for Bin Laden had come to an end and Donald Trump was just a hotel owner/reality TV host.

In the fifteen months it took me to write this book, I told myself I would never publish it, after all, the topics I cover are loaded with stigma and in some cases surrounded by a conspiracy of silence. But when the manuscript was ready, I pressed send and felt a wave of relief that I had taken control of my personal narrative for the first time in my life. The judgment I feared never materialized, but support, encouragement and validation did.

In the intervening years since its publication, I've watched study after study come out in support of what my lived experience had already confirmed: that mental illness is rooted in the seat of the emotions, that it is inextricably intertwined with stressful events that happen in our lives, and that the treatment is far more complex than a prescription of talk therapy and pharmaceutical drugs.

In fact, the prescription is more closely related to mountain sports (i.e. activities that bring us into the present moment and ground us in our bodies) than I ever could have imagined when I was introduced to ice climbing while I was still addicted to street drugs. Since my book was released, nature bathing and wilderness therapy have sprung up as healing modalities in their own right. Doctors in Scotland now prescribe nature as a cure for many ills, and movement is scientifically proven to be the most natural and safe means of elevating the level of neurotransmitters in the brain. All this to say that far from discovering anything new, I had inadvertently stumbled upon something as age-old as humanity itself.

The genesis of this book occurred in the Mountain and Wilderness Writing Program at the Banff Centre for the Arts. I had gone there to write a book about the tragic loss of a climbing partner, and instead emerged with the bones of an inner journey so personal I wasn't sure I could ever share it with the world.

I will forever be grateful to Diane Morriss at Sono Nis Press for taking my project on and allowing me to retain control over a very personal story. When her warehouse burned down and she gave me back the rights to my book, the only solution seemed to be to self-publish under my own banner.

Until I met Don Gorman at Rocky Mountain Books and felt the same level of trust that I had with Diane.

The book you are holding in your hands has a history befitting the journey described in these pages: it has literally risen from the ashes and been reborn.

MARGO TALBOT
NOVEMBER 2019
CANMORE, ALBERTA

ACKNOWLEDGMENTS

I WOULD LIKE TO THANK all of my psychologists, psychiatrists, and clinical social workers, particularly Elaine Spencer, who seemed to understand me as though she had lived my life. Everyone mentioned in this book, whether they appear as saints or sinners, helped me grow in ways I never would have had I not encountered them in the exact form and at the exact time that I did. Though certain names have been changed and circumstances altered to protect certain people, they are forever imprinted on my soul for their contributions to the person I have become.

Life has been my greatest teacher, aided and abetted by the best minds in trauma healing and spiritual transformation: Bessel van der Kolk, Gabor Maté, Eckhart Tolle, and Caroline Myss.

Thanks to Rocky Mountain Books for giving my memoir its second wind. If my book ever gets judged by its cover, Paul Zizka gets the credit for gracing the world with unparalleled mountain photography, and Chyla Cardinal for turning his image into a cover more beautiful than I ever could have imagined.

Special thanks goes out to Ken Wallator, who lost his battle with darkness, but gave me the gift that keeps on giving...

PROLOGUE

THE STAGE

As I stood on top of Mount Vinson, the highest peak in Antarctica, I was overcome by a sense of inner joy. It was February 2006—a lifetime away from what I now realize was the turning point in my life. As I watched Rob, my client and climbing partner, take photos from the summit, my mind drifted back to March 1992.

The cop who had busted me stood outside my cell door, throwing his keys into the air and catching them over and over again. "We know who you're involved with, and we know why you take all those trips out to the coast. You're not fooling us with your story. We've got enough information to put you away for a really long time." I ignored him. If the cops knew as much as he said they did, I would be looking at a serious prison sentence. But maybe he was bluffing, trying to get me to break down and rat on somebody higher up the ladder. He eventually left me to contemplate what my life had boiled down to.

The view from Mount Vinson was breathtaking, even as memories cascaded through my mind, taking me back through the decades of my depression and addiction, of breakdowns and therapy. I was surrounded by the things that had given me the greatest solace during those times: nature in general and mountains in particular. There had been a time when rage and pain, fuelled by a childhood of neglect and abuse, were all that I knew. Getting thrown in jail turned out to be a blessing in disguise, because it became the impetus to turn around and face that pain. It was the hardest thing I had ever done in my life, but the most worthwhile. I chose to undo the damage and begin again with choices I'd never had as a child. I decided that the events of my past could only control me if I let them, and this I would no longer do.

Novelist Tom Robbins said that it is never too late to have a happy childhood, and I am living proof of that. Now I go to drugstores to buy glitter makeup and bubble gum, spend my leisure time actively in fresh air, and dance for hours at parties because I'm just happy to be alive. My friends are not addicts, I don't live on the street, and my parents exist in a faraway mist that no longer rules my life. I have known darkness and have chosen the light.

My mind returned to the present and the minus-fifty-degree temperature that was its defining feature. I motioned to Rob that we needed to begin our descent to the shelter of high camp. He had conquered Mount Vinson, the sixth peak in his bid to do the seven summits. This climb meant a lot to Rob, I was certain. But I was just as certain that he had no idea what it meant to me.

1

ECHO MADNESS

A FULL MOON HUNG IN THE SKY on the night I was born. March 27, 1964, was also the day an earthquake rocked the west coast of Alaska. I popped out on the opposite side of the continent, in Fredericton, the capital city of New Brunswick. Although my parents had prayed for a boy, I emerged as their third daughter. Karla was three months shy of her third birthday when I was born, and Jane was sixteen months old. My mother picked my name from a list of bingo winners she saw on TV, removing the silent *t* at the end of "Margot."

"It was superfluous, and therefore pretentious," she told me years later. "Besides, I didn't want people to think you were French."

French like my father. Born in Quebec City, he spent his early childhood there, until his mother became too ill to care for him and his three siblings. At the age of four he was put into a Catholic orphanage in New Brunswick and never saw his parents again. His mother was French-Canadian, and his father was described as a drunken sailor or a drunken Indian, depending on who you talked to. My grandmother had run off with him when she was seventeen, and her family had disowned her. After she died, the family paid the church to destroy the birth records of her four children.

My parents didn't get too far into their marriage before my mother learned to wield these truths to her advantage. Whenever they argued, or whenever one of her daughters exhibited any untoward tendency, she would blame everything on the bad genes in my father's side of the family. And, the facts being what they were, he would have had a hard time defending either himself or his lineage.

My mother was a force to be reckoned with. She grew up in Minto, a small town that existed solely as a creation of a coal-mining company. Her father was a miner, and her mother had a greater capacity for churning out children than she had for taking care of them. My mother was the eldest, and she stepped in as surrogate mother to her nine siblings.

My parents met in 1960 and fell madly in love. My father worked for the Department of Agriculture in animal husbandry, and my mother was putting herself through nursing school. They seemed the perfect couple: my dad was tall, dark, and handsome, and my mother was considered the beauty of her high school graduating class. But the seeds of their future problems were as firmly planted in their psyches as they were invisible to the outside world.

My parents took a two-week road trip when I was five months old. My father was restless, and his nerves weren't strong enough to allow him to be around us kids much, so he convinced my mother that the drive would be a good break for them. My mother found a woman from a neighbouring town who would look after her daughters, and with that my parents set off on their trip. When they returned ten days later, they dismissed the babysitter. The next morning, when my mother came into my bedroom, I lay motionless in my crib and showed no sign that I recognized her. My mother could not get me to make eye contact with her or respond to her in any way. Weeks went by before she could get me to smile.

When I was a year old, my parents bought a house in Riverview, a small town about two hours away from Fredericton. My dad was glad to leave his job with the government—it was too predictable and had become boring to him. Instead, he figured he'd try his hand at being an insurance salesman. My mother refers to me as a model child during this time. She tells stories of how I was like a sack of potatoes on the floor. Whenever she put me down, I would not move from that spot; in fact I would barely play with my toys. In September 1966, when I was two and a half years old, my brother Frankie was born, and my parents finally had what they wanted: a boy.

One of my earliest memories is of a family visit to Oromocto in the spring of 1967. My mother's parents lived in this small town, a two-hour drive from Riverview, but we rarely visited. My grandparents didn't think much of my dad. They mistrusted him: he was an orphan, and therefore of dubious heritage. My father didn't feel welcome in their home, and all of us children felt the same way. As soon as we arrived, we were relegated to a back room to amuse ourselves while the grown-ups sat around the kitchen table imbibing their favourite adult beverages. The women were mostly teetotallers, but the men drank like there was no tomorrow. Billy, my mother's youngest brother, was especially renowned for his drinking prowess. Apparently he and his friends operated a still in the woods behind their childhood home from the time he was eleven. Roseanne, my mother's sister, was the one relative who took any notice of us when we visited, and she would make a fuss over us the likes of which we had never seen.

On the early visit that I remember, I had just turned three. Roseanne and I were alone in the house except for Uncle Billy, who was watching TV in the living room. We were in the kitchen, where I was helping her make "mini-pizzas"—slices of bread covered with ketchup and chopped-up hot dogs. When Roseanne discovered we had run out of cheese, she called to Billy, telling him that she needed to step out for a few minutes and that he should watch me while she was gone. Twenty minutes later she returned to find Billy chasing me around the kitchen with a ten-inch butcher's knife in his hands. While I was screaming, he was laughing maniacally. As Roseanne ran over to pick me up, she yelled at him, "You useless drunk! Can't we trust you to do anything right?" He continued laughing, but at least he put away the knife.

In the far corner of our kitchen, a bench was set up in such a way that there was only a narrow opening between the bench and the wall. I would cover this gap with a blanket and crawl inside. I dragged other loose blankets and pillows in there and brought my stuffed tiger in to keep me company. This was my hiding place, my secret fort. Tiger and

I spent hours in that fort, playing and napping and talking about what life would be like when I grew up. We dreamed about all the places we would visit and the people we would meet. Mostly I was left alone while I was in there, except when Mom would get down on her knees, come to the opening, and try to coax me out. She said it wasn't good for me to be spending so much time alone—I should be playing with the other kids in the neighbourhood, or at least getting some fresh air.

Mom started locking me out of the house to encourage me to play outside, but it didn't work—I just hung on to the door handle, crying and begging her to let me back inside. I was confused: I didn't want to play with other kids, and fresh air meant nothing to me compared with the peace and quiet of my secret hiding place. Still, by the time I was five I had traded the fort in the kitchen for real forts in the woods behind the house. At first I went there with Peter, a boy from the neighbourhood. We would build forts out of branches and leaves and play inside these for hours. Eventually, though, I found myself alone in the woods, venturing farther from the house and building shelters on my own.

When I started school in the fall of 1970, my mother enrolled me in the first French-immersion program in the country. My teacher was an Acadian nun who lived across the river. I was an intelligent child and I loved school; I especially loved it when Sister Legere came around to review my homework, something she did every day. Each time she stopped by my desk, I could tell she was pleased. I was a dutiful child who took my studies seriously because I knew that one of the only ways I could get my mother's approval was to get good grades. I'd had nothing but straight A's since I started school.

I liked Sister Legere. She was calm and gentle, and one day she asked me questions about my life at home. I was happy that she was taking an interest in me, though I didn't know how to answer most of her questions. She put a big blue star on my paper and smiled at me. Just before she left my desk, she gently brushed my hair away from my face, and I could feel myself freeze up inside. I couldn't remember the last time I had been touched in this way. Although I pretended everything was normal, I could feel my face getting hot as an unidentifiable feeling rose up in me. Luckily there were many students in the class, and within moments Sister Legere had moved on to the desk behind mine.

With each passing year, it became clearer to my sisters and me that my little brother Frankie was my mother's favourite. She spent most of her time with him when she was not cooking or cleaning the house. If any of us mentioned this, she would tell us that Frankie needed her more than we did because he was a boy and did not pick up on things as quickly as we did.

One day when I came home from school, Mom was sitting on the couch reading a book to him. I paused in the hallway as I watched them cuddled up on the couch. Frankie looked over and caught my eye. He turned back to her and said, "Mom, how come Margo never smiles?"

There was a moment of silence before she replied, "Oh, I don't know. Some people just don't smile as much as others. It doesn't mean they're not happy."

I learned when I was young that expressing my needs only got me into trouble. My mother ruled the household with her eyes, and I became adept at avoiding her ocular daggers. My feelings at that time were of overwhelming sadness. I felt alone and had already learned that it was futile to try to reach out to my parents. The only way to gain my mother's approval was to bring home good grades and help her with her chores. My parents owned apartment buildings near where we lived, and from the time I started school I was helping my mother clean them after school and on weekends.

This contrasted wildly with the treatment my brother received from my parents, and it was more and more obvious to my sisters and me that he was their pride and joy. It seemed like Mom only spoke to us to tell us how to pick up after ourselves or which chores needed to be done. When we asked her why Frankie never had to do any chores, she told us that boys took longer to mature than girls or that their arm muscles didn't develop as early, and that would be the end of the conversation. When Frankie started school, my mother sat with him every night and helped him with his homework. Early on, my sisters developed an attitude of not caring, but for years I continued trying to win my mother's approval.

Dad relied on Mom to do the parenting. The abandonment he had endured as a child had deeply scarred him. He had no idea how to raise kids, having no role models to draw on, and his temper prevented his disciplining us in any balanced way. He began finding ways to be away from home, first through work and then by helping neighbours with chores—fixing their roofs and mowing their lawns. Eventually he found solace in going out drinking with his friends.

By the time I was in Grade 2, my father was working as a travelling salesman, selling vacuum cleaners. He was always on the road, which is where he preferred to be. Whenever he was home he would tell stories about how he sold vacuum cleaners to lonely old women, farmers' wives, or schoolteachers, who would often cook him a meal and give him a place to stay for the night.

Dad was great at his job: every year he would win the "salesman of the year" award as well as every prize in between. (This was how I got my first bike—a pink single-speed with a banana seat and ape handles. I was seven, and it took me days to figure out how to ride it on the street in front of our house.) He also won many trips, mainly to popular resorts such as Florida and the Bahamas, so he and my mother regularly went on vacations. It wasn't easy to find someone to babysit four children for two weeks, but my mother always managed to find someone via word of mouth.

In twenty years of therapy, I learned two things that I believe to be immutable laws of psychology: depression is repressed anger, and anger is repressed sadness. At some point in my early years I learned to stuff all of my pain deep inside, but it was only a matter of time before this was bound to surface in some way.

The first time I remember acting out my anger was when I was seven years old. I was sitting in Dad's favourite chair, a black leather reclining armchair that was in the living room close to the front door. I had a pad of paper in one hand and a pen in the other. My parents were supposed to return from their latest trip to Barbados that day, and they were late. I was upset that they had gone away and left us in the care of yet another complete stranger. I felt like my parents didn't care about me, that they were too busy to spend time with my sisters and me when they were home, and that they spent any leisure time they did have away from us.

I put the pen in my left hand, with the tip facing downward, and began to lift my arm up, then let it drop down, rhythmically poking holes in the armrest of the chair. When the armrest on my left was full of little holes, I switched the pen to my right hand and repeated the action on the other side. My parents arrived in the driveway only a few minutes after I had finished disfiguring the chair. I knew what I had done was wrong, so I got out of the chair and pretended to be playing with some toys as they walked in the door. It was hours before my mother noticed the chair. She asked each of us children who had done such a thing. At first I stayed silent, but eventually I had to tell her it was me.

"But why would you do such a thing?" she asked, reasonably enough. "You know that's your father's favourite chair."

I lifted my shoulders up to my ears and lowered them again. My anger welled to the surface, and I tried to hide it. I stayed silent, but inside my mind I was screaming: *How come you only notice me when I'm doing something wrong?*

One of my favourite TV shows was *Grizzly Adams*. The show's main character, a frontiersman living in exile in the mountains, was the first man I actually envisioned myself living with when I got older. I loved his ruggedness and his self-sufficiency, traits I wanted to emulate. It wasn't lost on me that he bathed only when he wanted to, and then only in a stream or a lake. I had always hated having to bathe, and I was astonished to learn that I would need to perform regular body maintenance for my entire life: not just bathing, but brushing my teeth, combing my hair, and shaving my legs.

Around this time I realized it was unusual for a mother to still be in bed when her children returned home from school in the afternoon. I didn't piece this together on my own but learned it from dialogue I overheard in the schoolyard. Other girls my age talked about the things they would do with their mothers—helping to cook, going shopping after school or on weekends. My mother didn't do any of these things with me. Instead, she would rise from her bed around four in the afternoon and open the heavy curtains that kept out the daylight. She would walk down the stairs to the kitchen, where she would smoke cigarettes and listen to the radio. My mother was interested in just about every program broadcast on the CBC. And because she slept all day, she would be up all hours of the night, listening to radio shows and cleaning and vacuuming the house. Up to this point, I had thought this was the way things were for every family. But once I realized that this was not the case, I began taking more notice of it. I remembered a time when my mother did seem to be up when I got home from school, or was only occasionally still in bed, but I couldn't remember how long ago that was. I now began wondering about it, but I knew enough not to ask.

When I was ten I contracted pneumonia. My mother, a nurse, decided that it was just a chest cold, so after a few days off from school I was sent back to classes. My cough persisted and eventually got worse, and the teacher sent me home again. I was frightened by the coughing spells because it was becoming hard for me to breathe. My coughing displaced so much liquid in my chest that when I tried to inhale, it simply rolled around in my chest, causing a tickling sensation in my lungs that would start a whole new round of coughing. One morning I went into such a coughing fit at home that I thought I was going to die. There was nobody else in the house, and I was more frightened than I had ever been in my life.

Later that evening, as I lay in bed coughing, I heard my father pleading with my mother to take me to the hospital. "That's no normal cough, Sheila, and she's been out of school for weeks now." My mother insisted that it was nothing, that it would be gone soon enough.

I still had the cough ten months later. Finally my mother gave in and took me to a doctor.

"How long has your daughter had this cough?" he asked after he had finished examining me.

I noticed my mother tense up at the question. "Well, I guess it started about ten months ago," she replied.

The doctor's eyebrows went up, and his forehead furrowed. "She's in the latter stages of pneumonia, so the worst is over," he said with some restraint. "I'll write out a prescription for penicillin, which should take care of the rest of it."

My mother couldn't leave the doctor's office fast enough, and not a word was spoken between us about the past ten months of illness.

Later that evening, I overheard the conversation between my parents. My father's voice carried through the house: "For Christ's sake, Sheila, you're a nurse! How the hell do you mistake pneumonia for a common cold?"

My mother replied in her cold and dismissive tone, "I don't care what you think, Frank. There is no way anyone could have known that she had anything other than a common cold."

Dad offered me my first beer a few months later. He drank a brand called Alpine, whose label featured a beautiful graphic of a snow-covered mountain. After opening a bottle, he poured most of it into a glass for me and handed the remainder, in the bottle, to Frankie. This didn't go over well with my mother, but Dad thought he was teaching me how to handle my liquor. "Do you want her learning how to drink out on the streets, Sheila, or here at home where she is safe?" I didn't pay much attention to their fighting; I was too busy appreciating my first glass of beer. I loved it. I'm not sure if it was the taste, the effect of the alcohol, or simply the fact that I felt really grown up having more than just a sip of the golden beverage.

Shortly after this I remember finding a *Cosmopolitan* magazine lying around the house. I flipped through it and discovered an interview with Katherine Hepburn. In the article, Katherine spoke of how she liked to live her life as a man would, with all of the attendant freedoms. In the accompanying photo, she was sitting in a lounge chair in faded jeans and a white-collared shirt, her hair unbrushed. I decided there and then that I too was going to live my life as men did, and that I wasn't going to waste my time caring about how I looked. I flipped through the remainder of the magazine and realized that the models who appealed to me most were the ones with windblown hair, not the ones who were perfectly coiffed.

My father loved Western movies, and as a result I grew up seeing just about every Western that was ever made. "I was born in the wrong century," Dad would exclaim, to no one in particular, both during and after every film. Apparently *The Godfather* fit into his exclusive club of respectable movies, and when I was eleven we watched it on the television in the living room together. Although I vividly remember being shocked by the scene with the horse's head in the bed, I otherwise loved the film. The scenes were exotic and the characters vivid.

A few weeks later my father asked me, out of nowhere, "Margie, what do you want to do when you grow up?"

Without a moment's hesitation I replied, "I'm going to live in the mountains and work for the Mafia."

"Well," my father replied, "you'd better be careful. Those guys are dangerous."

My mother hated cooking and had a quick recipe that she would often make us for dinner: "meal in a dish." She would open a few cans of Campbell's tomato soup, throw in some hamburger and whatever vegetables were in the freezer, turn the burner on low, and let the concoction simmer over the next two hours. Once it was ready, we were free to come into the house and eat. Since there was no schedule, we rarely sat down to dinner together as a family.

In April 1975, one month after I turned eleven, my parents made a point of telling us that we would be eating in the dining room at six that evening and that we all had to be there. As we were used to running our own schedules, this was no small feat to accomplish. We met in the dining room at the appointed time, just as Mom was serving up spaghetti and meatballs on the "nice" table usually reserved for adult company. Once we were all seated and ready to eat, Mom and Dad told us that they had an announcement to make. After an awkward preamble, Dad said, "Your mother is pregnant. She's going to have another baby in a few months. She'll need your help with this, so I expect you to help her."

I had no idea what he was talking about. His speech sounded like a bunch of abstract words. But over the next few months, as I watched my previously limber mother barely make it up the stairs to her bedroom, I began to understand what my father was trying to tell us—to tell me—although I was still unsure how I could possibly be of any help. My mother, now thirty-seven, was on the cusp of having her fifth child. It was clear that she could barely take care of the children she already had, let alone add another one to the brood.

Five months later, Richard was born. From the moment Mom brought him home from the hospital, he was the joy of my life—so much so that I felt he had been born just for me. I no longer felt alone; his arrival created a level of well-being that I had never experienced before. My two sisters had already entered puberty and had lives outside our home that left little room for the family. In contrast, I was a loner. I had no friends, so Richard became the centre of my universe. It was late September when he was born, so I was back in school, but I spent all my time after school and on weekends with him. He was cute and funny, and by the time he started to walk, he strode around like a miniature football player. I took him everywhere with me, and I liked being around him more than I did anyone my own age. When my mother wasn't in bed she doted on Richard as much as she did on Frankie. But that didn't bother me. My days of trying to win her approval were quickly coming to an end.

2

WILD FIRE

MY SISTER JANE RECENTLY TOLD ME that our family was always afraid
of my anger. I can't remember exhibiting it in my younger years, but I do
remember the day the power dynamic shifted between my mother and me.
It was the summer after I turned twelve. I was upstairs having a fight
with Karla and must have used some of the colourful new words the boys
on the street had taught me, because the next thing I knew my mother was
coming up the stairs with a brush in her hand. When she reached the landing, energy that I had never felt before welled up inside me. I grabbed the
brush from her, throwing it over her head and down the stairs. My mother
looked shocked, and I was prepared to physically fight her if I had to. She
was staring straight into my eyes, and I could see she was afraid of me. This
was the first time I was aware of the power of my anger. I realized this was
the key to pushing back the oppressive world that had been closing in on
me since I was born.

When I realized that my mother could no longer control me, I ran wild.
The shift happened so quickly that my mother thought (and still thinks)
that I went crazy. But in my view, this was my first step toward breaking
free from constantly trying to win her approval. Before, I had been a quiet,
obedient child; now, suddenly, I began living out on the streets, drinking,
doing drugs, and hanging out with older boys. Dad threatened to send me
to a foster home so that I could learn to appreciate having a family, and

Mom wanted to call the cops. But they could only pretend to discipline me, as I was completely beyond anyone's control.

I laughed in their faces and cried behind their backs. Now I know that, deep down, I just wanted love, and because I wasn't getting it at home, I went looking for it in the streets. At the time, I was completely unaware of the reasons for my behaviour. I supported my habits by bootlegging to minors with the help of some older boys. I was kicked off every sports team in school, but I didn't care: the world was fucked, and I was hell-bent on breaking every one of its rules.

While my code of conduct around my parents was silence, my behaviour elsewhere spoke volumes. My tribe of dispossessed children became my family, and I began to live by my own laws—laws that sprang from the unspoken anger that was always just below the surface.

My sisters, Karla and Jane, weren't faring much better, although their behaviour was certainly more subtle than mine. Karla, now fifteen, had her first real boyfriend, Donnie, and she spent all of her time with him or his family. Jane was either acting in school plays or locked in her room, reading tomes like Freud's *Interpretation of Dreams*. Even though I was breaking more rules than either of them, my sisters bore the brunt of Mom's disciplinary zeal.

I was thirteen years old the first time Donnie bought beer for me and my friends. He had given me a ride and dropped me off with a case of twenty-four beers, and I was waiting at the end of a residential road where I had arranged to meet up with a few male friends. I didn't have any female friends then. Most girls my age were obsessed with fashion, makeup, and boys, but I had no interest in those things. I had begun to notice how these girls' behaviours changed when they were around members of the opposite sex, and I wanted no part of that. It was as if they became more concerned with what the boys thought than with what they themselves thought. I felt these girls would betray me in a heartbeat if it meant winning the approval of one of the boys. I saw it as deceitful at best and dangerous at worst and decided I was not going to play that game.

The boys and I had discovered a shack between the fairways of the local golf course, and we adopted it as our hangout. This particular day was late in the fall, so we had brought along some candles for warmth as well as light. As we came out of the wooded area and onto the fairway, it seemed like a long way to walk with the weight of a two-four of beer on my shoulder. I shifted the box onto my left shoulder, and the guys waited for me. Halfway across the fairway I heard voices. I looked over and saw two men out for some late-season golf. They seemed astonished at the sight of us on their golf course, but I shot them an angry glance and they left us alone.

We got to the shack and went inside. There wasn't much there—just some sort of mechanical device and a few boxes. We positioned the boxes like chairs around a table, with the largest box serving as a surface for our candles and drinks. As we drank, we laughed and talked. Tom updated us on the rum he was making in his bedroom closet and promised to pass the recipe along if his experiment was a success. Nick talked about racing cars and how much he looked forward to the freedom of having his own one day. Although I was a few years younger than they were, we all swore that we would get our driver's licences on the day we turned sixteen.

I told them about my basketball coach, who threatened to kick me off the team if I didn't stop hanging around with people who drank and did drugs.

"What did you do?" Tom asked.

"I never showed up for another practice," I replied. I could tell that they thought it was cool how I had handled the situation, and I loved the feeling I got when I saw their nods of approval. If we had anything in common it was our contempt for authority, whether in the form of parents, teachers, or the law. We didn't live in healthy homes, with parents who wanted to know where their children were and what they were doing. On the contrary, nobody noticed that we regularly went out drinking and smoking pot.

We had been in the shack for about an hour when we heard a noise outside. We knew that there was never anyone on the fairway after the golfers had finished their rounds, so we stopped talking and listened. My mind flashed back to the two men we'd encountered on our way over, and I realized they had called the police.

"It's the cops," I whispered.

I didn't wait for the guys to make a move. I was out the door and running into the woods before anyone could stop me. I was a strong runner and knew that I could outrun the police. I looked back only once and saw their flashlights waving into the night. I heard men's voices yelling at me to stop, but I paid no attention. I ran parallel to the fairway until I was far enough away to feel safe out in the open. When I reached the road, I slowed down to a walk and pretended I was just a kid wandering the streets at night. It was too dark for the cops to have gotten a good look at me, and if confronted I knew I could lie my way out of it.

Around this time my parents decided to sell the apartment buildings they owned because they were too much work for my mother. Although she was getting up earlier during the week when there was no one else around to look after Richie, she did not have enough energy for anything other than looking after the basics. Mom and Dad put the proceeds from the sale into a joint bank account. My father then decided it was time to start his own sales company and began importing Volta vacuum cleaners from Sweden. Having no business experience or office skills, he hired a secretary, and within months she had embezzled all the funds in their account. Out of money, Dad moved to Saint John, where he got a job managing an apartment building. Mom often travelled there to visit him on weekends; sometimes she took my brothers with her, but often she left them at home with my sisters and me. By this time Jane had a boyfriend, Mark, and she spent as much time with him as Karla did with Donnie. While my older sisters hung out with their boyfriends, I would throw huge parties at the house. Despite my best efforts to clean up afterward, my mother would sometimes find a broken light fixture or discarded beer cap behind a chair. She would immediately confront Karla and Jane, but when they told her to ask me, she backed down. I don't know if she thought the idea of a thirteen-year-old throwing parties was ludicrous, or if she was simply afraid of my anger.

My mother finally tired of the travelling and decided she would move us all to Saint John so that we could be together. She timed our move for the fall of 1978, when I was starting Grade 9 and my two older sisters were in high school. We moved into the apartment building my dad managed. My parents and the boys lived in one unit on the fifteenth floor, while Karla and Jane lived in another unit on the ground floor. I floated in between. Although my bedroom was in the upstairs apartment, I spent most of my time downstairs, hanging out with my two older sisters.

Frankie and Richard quickly found new friends in Saint John, but my sisters and I did not. In the year that it took to sell the house in Riverview, Karla, Jane, and I regularly travelled back there on weekends and school holidays to visit friends and, in my case, to party. I was still not one of the popular kids, but I was accepted by the wilder teenagers who hung out on the fringes and led infinitely more adventurous lives. With these kids as my peers, I became the kind of teenager other mothers feared to let their daughters hang around. This suited me just fine. I had now decided that I preferred the company of men. Among the boys, I was renowned for my ability to put away vast quantities of alcohol. There are many nights from this time that I have no memory of at all.

My mother blamed her daughters' lack of friends in Saint John on the fact that she had moved us at such a vulnerable age. Whenever she mentioned this I felt like asking: "Then why the hell did you move us?"

Two months after we had moved to Saint John, I was back at the house in Riverview. It was November, and the chill of the oncoming winter was hanging in the air. I had just left the house and was walking to meet my friends at a party. It was already dark, and on this particular night I was feeling very lost and alone. The sky was clear and there were a million stars directly over my head. I loved how they shone and sparkled, how they seemed so alive in the night air. I slowed down, and as I looked up at the stars a feeling of overwhelming sadness came over me. I thought to myself: *I have no parents; I have nobody to take care of me.*

This feeling was not new, but my direct acknowledgment of it was. I had always felt alone in the world, as though I were suspended in a void and completely disconnected from others, even when I was in their midst. I had never confronted this feeling before, and it unnerved me to feel the depth of my emotional barrenness.

"We're your parents, and we will always take care of you."

This response was as clear as if the words had been spoken into my ear. I stopped, and the world stood still as I stared up at the sky and the multitude of glittering jewels of light stared back at me. I felt as though the stars had spoken directly to me, and I instantly felt a comfort beyond words. I knew that what they were telling me was true: they would always be watching over me.

Although I usually took the bus or hitchhiked to Riverview, sometimes I went with my father when he was returning there on business. Exactly what the nature of this business was, we were never quite sure. One weekend I was getting ready to catch a ride with him. I had thrown together the bare necessities for the trip, and as I was about to go out the door, my mother handed me a twenty-dollar bill. It was rare for her to give me any money. She told me it was for food, so that my father and I could eat something while we were away.

I took the money and hopped into the car. Dad put on the only tape he owned, *The Best of Johnny Cash*, and we navigated the back roads out to the highway that connected Moncton and Saint John. Half an hour later my father turned off the highway at the town of Sussex and pulled into a liquor store. As our car approached the store, we could see two parking spots, side by side, and another car entering the lot directly in front of us. The driver pulled up right in the middle of those two spots, straddling them in such a way that we could not fit in either of them. Dad banged his fists on the steering wheel and yelled, "Fuck! What an idiot!"

I was uncomfortable, not because he had sworn—I was no stranger to any of that—but because I didn't like to be alone with him when his anger surfaced. When he finally found a place to park, he gestured to me with his open hand.

I asked, "What do you want?"

He said, "You know, the money your mother gave you back at the house. Give it to me, I need it."

I was stunned that he knew about the money. Mom had handed it to me as Dad was walking out the door and had whispered when she told me what it was for. It occurred to me to lie, to say that she hadn't given me anything, that he must be mistaken. But I remembered his temper, and I handed over the money.

When Dad got back into the car, he handed me a brown paper bag containing a bottle of Bacardi rum and pulled back onto the highway. I knew the ritual well; I had been performing it for many years. I opened up one of the cans of Coke that he always kept in the car, took a big swig, and then poured rum in the can until the drink was up to its original level. I handed the can over to Dad, keenly aware of the sticker on the back window: *Don't Drink and Drive.*

In January 1979 Karla announced that she was seven months pregnant. I had already figured it out, so I was stunned that it was news to my parents. Mom announced that she was hauling all of us to a family psychologist. She wanted my dad to come as well, but he flat out refused. She thought there was something wrong with her children, specifically with her three daughters, and the surprise pregnancy only confirmed it for her. We were unresponsive to her, and she couldn't figure out why. Apparently she didn't know that teenagers are not into hour-long monologues on how they should behave, especially when the monologue is not communicated respectfully. She was also unaware that if you ignore the needs of your children long enough, they will eventually learn to ignore you too. So one afternoon we all got in the car and headed over to Dr. Gibson's office in downtown Saint John.

Dr. Gibson ushered us into a room where he had arranged seven chairs in a circle. After we had all seated ourselves, he sat in the empty chair, said hello to each of us, and went around the circle getting us to introduce ourselves. We had never been to anything so formal, so we sat up straight and paid attention.

Dr. Gibson began by asking my mother a few questions, such as what she thought might be happening in our family and why she had brought us there. Then he did something that I thought was very strange at the time but that I now know to be brilliant. He went around the circle and asked each child the same three questions: "When was the last time your mother touched you? When was the last time your mother gave you a hug? When was the last time your mother told you she loved you?"

I don't remember what my two brothers answered, but I do remember what we three girls said: none of us could remember ever being touched, hugged, or told that we were loved.

Dr. Gibson turned to my mother and said, "Sheila, you're like a robot with your daughters. You tell them how to put the dishes away and when to brush their teeth, but you don't show them any emotion, any love. Above all else, children need love."

My mother was now extremely uncomfortable. She had brought us here thinking that everything was my father's fault, or our fault, but she had never thought that anything could be *her* fault. When the hour was up, she whisked us out of the office. She never mentioned the visit, nor did she ever take us to another professional to find out what was wrong with our family. I believe that Dr. Gibson knew this would be her reaction, and he used that hour to get a message across to us girls: You are worthy of love, even if your mother doesn't show you any affection.

Two months later, Karla gave birth to a healthy baby girl at the Saint John General Hospital. Mom and Dad were out of town somewhere, so Donnie's parents came to visit her right before the birth. On the advice of Donnie's mother, Karla gave the child up for adoption. I took the bus downtown to visit her as often as I could. We were not a close family, and I had no idea what to say. But I was able to ask her if she needed anything and promised I would bring it with me if I could.

That fall I started high school. I had always managed to tune out other kids, but high school was a whole other beast. I was considered strange by my contemporaries, and they spread rumours about me: I was a lesbian, I sold drugs, I would do anything with any boy to get my hands on drugs. The clothes I wore—handed-down overalls with patches, and my father's flannelette shirts—did not help things. I was dubbed "the farmer's daughter," and some kids laughed as they pointed me out in the hallways.

As far as I could tell we were poor, and I had learned not to ask for new clothes. So I was surprised one day, while standing in the kitchen, to overhear my parents arguing in the next room. "Take her shopping, for Christ's sake, Sheila! You can't send a teenage girl to school looking like that. She'll be an outcast." I couldn't hear my mother's reply, but I did hear my father pleading, "Take her tonight; get her something that a normal girl her age would wear."

As I listened I felt guilty, as I did for much of my childhood, for what I was costing my parents in terms of both energy and money. My mother had trained her girls not to have any needs and not to make any waves. So I was surprised by my father's show of support and touched that he had not only noticed but had the courage to confront my mother about it. I secretly hoped that she would take me shopping, not just because I might get some proper clothes, but also because I would interpret this as a sign that she cared for me. But we didn't go shopping that night, or any night, and I soon forgot all about it.

Ever since I had entered puberty, I would cry uncontrollably about once each month, always in the privacy of my bedroom. I would be overcome with a great sadness, and when it became too strong to bear I would lock myself in my room, get under the covers of my bed, and sob until I felt empty. In Grade 10 my second-last period of the day was English. I looked forward to it all day long. I found that I could lose myself in literature: I related to the drama and intensity of these stories and would dream up adventures that I could become embroiled in when I too was an adult.

Sitting in English class one day, I felt the familiar emotion welling up inside me. I took out my notebook and, for the first time in my life, began writing down my turbulent thoughts and emotions. Although this helped, I could feel that the tide was too strong and that I was not going to make it home before the levee broke. Class was almost over. I decided that I would head to the principal's office and ask to see the nurse. I barely made it there and was sobbing as I walked into the principal's office. The secretary called the nurse, who took me into a tiny room nearby that had a cot. There was no conversation—I was much too upset to talk—so the nurse told me she would let me be and would come back before the end of the school day.

When she had left the room, I curled into a ball, my body heaving in rhythm with my sobs. The world disappeared, and I fleetingly wondered what the adults at the school were thinking of this development. Eventually I must have fallen asleep, because the next thing I knew, the bell had sounded and school was out. I lay there, wondering if my eyes were red and if the other students would be able to tell that something was up. But I needn't have worried. When the nurse came back in, we talked until all the students had left the building.

"Margo, do you want to talk about what is upsetting you?" she asked.

I just sat there. Other than mentioning my deep feelings of sadness, I didn't know what to tell her.

"Do you want me to call your parents?" she continued.

I didn't even have time to think. Now the words just flew out of my mouth: "No! Please don't call my parents."

She asked me if everything was okay at home, and I told her yes. We chatted while I got my notebooks together and ran my fingers through my hair. "Well," the nurse concluded, "if you ever need to talk about anything, just come by for a visit." I nodded and headed for the door.

Two months after this incident, Karla dropped out of high school and moved to Calgary with Donnie. Within a month, Jane moved to Moncton to live with Mark and his family, and three days after she left she called to tell us that she was pregnant and would be having her child in June. My parents were livid, but there was nothing they could do. My mother had never spoken to us girls about anything to do with womanhood, from the fact that we would be getting our periods to dating to birth control. What did she expect?

Within a month of Jane's leaving home, my father told me to get in the truck because we were going for a drive. It was not unusual for us to go for a drive and wind up at one of his friends' places, where I would be expected to keep myself busy while he had a few drinks. But on this day he drove into the countryside, found a quiet side road, and pulled into a clearing before turning off the engine. I sat in silence the whole way. I had no idea where we were going, or why, and I was not going to ask.

No sooner had my father turned off the ignition than he started to talk to me. He stared straight ahead. "I was waiting for your mother to tell you these things, but it's obvious she isn't going to, so I'm going to tell you myself." He paused. "I need to tell you this before you end up like Karla and Jane. You don't need to get pregnant. There are things you can do to prevent it. I hope at your age you're not in danger of this, but I need to make sure that when the time comes you know about all of your options. There are pills you can take that keep a woman from getting pregnant. You can get them from a doctor. If they won't give them to you, just come to me and I'll get them for you. It's too late now for Karla and Jane, but it's not too late for you. If you need anything, just come and ask me. I'll buy it for you. I'll give you money so you can get it yourself. All you have to do is ask."

And with that he started up the engine, and we drove back to town and to his friend Les's place. Les had a daughter who was my age, and we ran off together as soon as I hopped out of the truck. I was relieved to have a distraction from what had been an extremely uncomfortable exchange between my father and me. I knew he wouldn't have broached the subject if he were not so desperate to hold on to what remained of our family. It felt good to have finally had a real interaction with him, something I had never had before, but I also knew there was little chance that I would feel comfortable enough to take him up on his offer. Besides, I felt that I was in no danger of falling into the same condition as my sisters: I had decided to avoid sex like the plague. That afternoon in the truck was the only time either of my parents ever talked about sex to any of their children. In fact, it was the only time I remember getting any information on how to navigate life.

Jane came home for a visit one day in April 1980 when she was seven months pregnant. We were sitting on the couch most of the evening, talking about everything except what must have been foremost in her mind. Jane said that her stomach hurt, and she kept moving around to try to ease the pain. At one point my father's anger broke through, and he said, "What the hell do you expect, getting yourself into that situation? Of course your stomach is going to hurt!" My mother largely ignored Jane, but at eleven o'clock that night, with her daughter in tears and doubled over in pain, my mother capitulated and took her to the hospital.

As soon as the doctor had examined Jane, he rushed her into the operating room to remove her appendix. It had been about to burst. Not only did Jane's appendix come out that night, but so did her daughter, Erin. Jane stayed home for two weeks and then returned to Moncton to look for an apartment and try to figure out how to be a teenage mother. One month later we got a telephone call from Donnie: Karla had just given birth to a baby boy, and they had named him Jeffrey.

When summer vacation started, I went to Moncton to visit Jane. She had left Mark right after Erin was born, and now the reality of her situation was sinking in. She told me about the night she spent in the hospital after her delivery. A nurse had come in, sat down on her bed, and asked her if she had any idea how hard it was going to be to raise a child alone at such a young age. Jane thought the nurse was bitter, or jealous, and was trying to trick her into giving up her child. Now she understood.

"She was telling me the truth, Margo, and I wish I'd listened." She was crying as she spoke. "This is so much harder than I ever imagined it could be." She counselled me not to have a child unless I was prepared for my life to be difficult. I vowed that I would heed her advice.

My parents rarely spoke about my sisters after they became pregnant and left home, and they certainly didn't try to help them out. Karla had Donnie around for the first two years of Jeff's life, but Jane had no one to turn to. My sisters' absence was felt in our home, especially by me. I had lost my allies and was now the sole target for my parents' bitterness.

Shortly after I turned sixteen, I applied for a job and was hired at the local groceteria, the Village Mart. Teenage boys stocked shelves and unloaded trucks while girls ran the till and served from the bakery and the deli. I loved this job; it made me feel grown up and free to buy whatever I wanted with the money I earned. I enjoyed the friendship of the girls I worked with, and for the first time in my life I had a female peer group. My mother complained that my thirty-hour work weeks would lower my grades in school, but I ignored her as usual. The independence I had gained was well worth any sacrifice, and I began to realize that the more I was out of the house, the better I felt about myself.

Soon after I was hired, the groceteria took on another girl, Sarah. One night as we were cashing out she told me about her parents' troubled marriage and the distance between her and her brother. "I'm worried that they're not going to stay together," she confided of her parents' struggles. When I asked her if her brother felt the same way, she replied, "I can't discuss this with John; we barely talk to each other."

I was thrilled to be having such a heartfelt talk with another person. In my home we never spoke of our feelings, and my male friends never spoke of theirs, so a whole new world was opening up for me. Now I found that I couldn't wait to get home from school, or for the weekends to arrive, so I could be with Sarah and the other girls at work. I no longer saw myself as the black sheep of the family and the outcast at school. I felt accepted by my co-workers, and this acceptance, combined with a growing awareness of my body and my sexuality, was propelling me away from my family and into a new universe, where the power inside me was something greater than anger.

Shortly after I started work, I met Grant. He came into the Village Mart one Tuesday afternoon and chatted and flirted with me while I filled his order at the deli counter. I was flattered by the attention but thought little of it after he left. He returned the following day and asked me if I would like to go out on a date with him. He offered to pick me up on Friday evening after work, and I agreed.

Friday at work was much like any other; I was too naïve to be nervous. Grant picked me up at the appointed time in his mother's white Oldsmobile sedan. I noticed his clothes right away: he wore a new pair of jeans and a collared shirt, all much nicer than any clothing I owned. He was very clean and his hair was neatly brushed. I never brushed my hair, and for the first time in my life I became self-conscious about this. We drove to a Chinese diner and ordered sweet-and-sour rice dishes. I learned that Grant was a year older than I was and went to the same high school. He told me that he had just broken up with his first girlfriend because she wouldn't have sex with him. I had no intentions of having sex with him either, but I didn't tell him that. I was enjoying the attention too much to risk losing it so soon. We decided that night that we would start dating. I had my first real boyfriend.

It turned out that Grant's family was very wealthy compared to mine. His mother and sister put together care packages of clothing for me, and these were the nicest clothes I owned. To keep me from feeling too self-conscious, I think, they explained that they had outgrown the clothes, or simply had too many, and thought those clothes would look good on me.

From the time I started dating Grant, I felt I was learning how things worked in another world. When I first went to his mother's home for dinner, I had no idea what all the pieces of cutlery were for. I had grown up eating on my own most of the time and had developed some bad habits— including not using cutlery at all. Karla and I would joke that we loved having fingertip control of our food, but in Grant's home it was no joke.

Grant and my father hit it off right from the start. My mother, however, complained that Grant was controlling my every move. I knew even then that she was upset about losing her control over me, although she had in fact lost that a few years earlier. She would regularly comment on how much time I was spending with Grant, and usually at his place. She had felt the same way about Karla and Jane spending all their time at their boyfriends' places, and I chalked it up to her bruised ego rather than a desire that I spend more time at home.

Grant's parents were divorced, and his father owned a beautiful house on the other side of town. Whenever he was away, Grant and I would go over there and have small parties, either on our own or with a few other kids that we knew from school. It was in this house that I first had sex with Grant, who had been pressuring me about it since our first date. I told myself that it had to happen sooner or later, and I had had enough to drink that night to let down my guard. It was a very confusing time because I knew little about sex and was too freaked out at the idea of getting pregnant to enjoy it. Although my father had had that talk with me only months before, when the time came I felt too uncomfortable to discuss birth control with him.

For the next two decades, whenever I had sex with a man I would feel lost, as though I had no psychological boundaries and didn't know who I was or what I wanted. This would leave me dangerously vulnerable to the wishes of these men. At the same time, I came to understand the immense importance men placed on sex, and I saw this as a way to get the attention from them that I was not getting anywhere else in my life. Once I had gained enough experience to relax during sex, it became like another drug. Sex was the only time I would feel in the moment, connecting to both my own body and that of another living being.

3

BLESSED RAGE

A YEAR AND A HALF AFTER WE STARTED DATING, Grant left for Dalhousie University in Halifax and urged me to apply when the time came. We managed to keep up a long-distance relationship for the eight months he was gone, but it was time for me to make some decisions.

A few months before graduation, all the students at our high school were encouraged to meet with the guidance counsellor to discuss possibilities for the future. When I walked into the counsellor's tiny office, he motioned me to sit in the chair across from his desk. "What do you see yourself doing after you graduate?" he asked.

I told him, "I'm going to university to study languages and philosophy." I already had French as a second language, and my mother had put the idea in my head that I could be a translator. But the thing that intrigued me most was philosophy. Emotions felt dangerous to me. I seemed to get into trouble whenever I expressed them. So I was attracted to the cool rationality of logic, and I saw it as a safe guide out of my confusion in life.

The counsellor moved some papers around on his desk before looking up at me. "You'll never be able to find a job with that type of degree, unless you want to be a professor."

I didn't, and I also had no alternatives in mind. When I told him this, he suggested that I consider enrolling in business administration, which he considered the biggest career trend at the time.

I do not have many regrets in my life, but taking that advice is one of them. I knew better than anyone what most interested me, and I wish I'd had the strength to act on this. But the counsellor's was the only input I had—there was no one at home I could talk to about my decision. Although my mother was obsessed with the idea that she had to save Frankie from becoming a janitor, she had no interest in where her three daughters were headed. And my father felt threatened. He had quit school in Grade 8 to work on a farm and was insecure about his level of education. By the time my last year of high school was coming to an end, I couldn't wait to get out of the house, and I was too angry to even consider talking with my parents about my life choices.

I was accepted into Dalhousie University and enrolled in a bachelor of commerce program that began in September 1982. I got a student loan that paid for my tuition, and a bursary that paid for room and board in the women's dormitory. When I left home, both my sisters were struggling with single motherhood, trying to raise their kids with no help from their ex-partners, no money, and no family support. Still, we revelled in the fact that at least one of our childhood dreams had finally come true: we were out of our parents' home.

Grant was living in an apartment twenty minutes from campus. Sometimes I visited him during the week, but most often only on weekends. My penchant for partying got ramped up to a new level now that I was completely on my own. I found myself more at ease socially, and I soon began forming friendships outside Grant's orbit. I went to freshman functions and fraternity house parties almost every night. I had a high tolerance for liquor and rarely, if ever, suffered from a hangover.

A few months into my first semester I found out that all the women in my dorm were afraid of me: they thought I wanted to beat them up. It is true that I didn't have any respect for them or for what they wanted. I was initially rooming with a girl named Louise, and I found her so naïve that I didn't want anything to do with her. While most of the girls were away from their parents for the first time, I felt as though I had been on my own for years. For instance, the girls in the dorm made a big deal out of going out drinking, or staying out all night; these things had become commonplace for me.

I had brought my stereo with me, and the music I played was more raucous than that of the other girls. On one of my first nights in the dorm I came into the room drunk while Louise was playing one of her records on my stereo. I had no idea who the artist was, but it was some sort of slow and sappy love song. I walked over, lifted the needle off the vinyl, and asked, "What is this shit?" I then proceeded to put on the latest Rolling Stones album. Louise's friends left the room, but it barely registered with me. I had spent the past few years carefully constructing a tough shell around myself, and I was damned if I was going to let anybody break into it.

A week later I was returning from the cafeteria when Julia, another woman on our floor, flagged me down. "Hey, we're roommates now! Can you believe it?"

I could not believe it. Julia was the last person I would want to share a room with. She was loud and boisterous and seemed to like shocking people with her opinions on topics like sex. But when I announced that I already had a roommate, she told me that my roommate and hers had gone to see the dean because neither of them liked who they had been paired up with. And since Julia and I were the two women nobody else wanted to room with, we got to room together.

It turned out that we were perfect for each other. We had both arrived with beer fridges, loud stereos, and a penchant for wildness. I'm not sure how I kept my grades up; all I know is that I learned to study while drinking beer and listening to loud music. All through grade school I'd had an amazing memory, and this talent would be my best asset at university as well.

Julia was one of the few women I met who could keep up with me in the drinking department. We went to bars regularly, as well as going out dancing. Sometimes she would be in an intense relationship with a boyfriend and I wouldn't see her for a while, but then they would break up and we would be back in action. One evening we went to the Cosmo, the raciest dancing club in downtown Halifax. Julia and I were out on the dance floor when a song came on that I'd never heard before: Michael Jackson's "Billie Jean." I instantly adopted it as my favourite.

Julia and I got into regular trouble with the dean of our floor. We would listen to her admonishments in silence and then pity her for being so square as soon as she left the room. When the other girls chastised us for not helping them decorate the floor for the upcoming Christmas party, we promptly made cut-outs of penises and hung them up all over our room as well as in the hallways. Thus did we avoid future inclusion in any of their plans.

One afternoon we were in a bar with two of Julia's friends when one of them invited me to go to the women's room with her. Once there, she pulled out a purple cylindrical tab and asked if I wanted to drop acid. I was no stranger to drugs, but until then most of my experience had been with pot, hash and magic mushrooms. I must have looked perplexed, because Kate proceeded to describe what the high would be like, how long it would last, and what it would feel like to come down. It was clear to me that she was familiar with this drug. We decided to break the cylinder and do half a hit each.

Kate handed me my half and we each swallowed our portion. Back at our table we explained that we would need to leave the bar soon so that we would be in a more controlled atmosphere when the acid took over. We went back to Kate's apartment, sat on the floor, and chatted. Forty-five minutes later I was leafing through a magazine but still did not feel anything. Then, without warning, the magazine started to read like poetry and I had a hard time deciphering its meaning. I looked around the room. Everything had changed. Paintings on the wall became more vivid, textured, and rich. I looked at my hands and was fascinated by the lines on my palms and the colour of my fingernails. I caught Kate's eyes and we burst out laughing; it seemed we would never stop.

I went out on the balcony with a sense of euphoria the likes of which I had never felt before. I believed I finally understood what people meant by "happiness." There was a song playing on the radio, and I caught words from the refrain: "I'm walking on sunshine." I said to myself, "So am I!" I loved this feeling of emotional release from my normal state of anger and pain, and I wanted it to last forever. But drug trips do not last forever, and the only way to sustain the high was to do more of the drug. Which I did.

Soon after this I experienced another life-changing event. I had enrolled in a "theory of feminism" class as one of my electives. The professor, a lesbian in her thirties, was clearly angry at the power dynamic of the patriarchal paradigm. I enjoyed the class, and although the information was coloured by the professor's outrage, it made a lot of sense to me. One afternoon I arrived at the class to find the windows covered with dark cloth, and a screen in front of the chalkboard. The professor explained that we were going to be watching a documentary and warned that it might be disturbing. I walked to the back of the class, where I usually sat, and got comfortable.

The film, *Not a Love Story*, was about the pornography industry, its objectification of women, and its skewing of the psyches of men with respect to sex. It contained scenes of strippers and peep shows, skin magazines and films. Near the end it showed footage of pornographic films being made, beginning with soft porn and moving on to harder porn. This culminated in footage from a snuff film, where a woman was raped at gunpoint. The footage cut out just before she was shot, as the rapist reached orgasm. I had had very little exposure to porn, so much of this film was shocking to me. I felt violated just watching it. When the documentary ended, I was shaking and crying, and I remained in my seat until the other students had left the room. It was unusual for me to cry; I couldn't remember having done so since my episodes in puberty, but seeing that film opened a floodgate of emotion that I didn't know was inside me.

That night I was still numb from the experience. I could think of nothing but what I had seen in that film. Waves of emotion would come over me; I would begin to cry uncontrollably and then get myself together again, trying to function normally. The next day, as I sat through my classes, all I could think about was the final scene in the snuff film. I wondered who that woman was. How had she ended up in a snuff film? By the time classes ended, it was obvious to me that I needed to talk with someone, so I walked over to student services and asked if I could see a counsellor. I was led into a room where a woman sat behind a desk, and I broke down crying when she asked me why I had come to see her. We talked for an hour, and I felt better when I left. But I knew something huge had been triggered inside me. I also knew that I didn't have a clue what it was.

Nothing was the same after this. I became more introspective, and I began looking at people differently. I also started to notice incidents that made me reflect on the differences between my family and the families of the other girls in my dorm. These were not only incidents I observed first-hand, such as their lengthy telephone calls home, made from the payphone down the hall. There were also conversations when I heard the girls talk about how much they missed their parents. I never missed mine. I became uncomfortable listening to them describe their visits home, when they would have their favourite home-cooked meals or go out shopping with their mothers. I couldn't handle my feelings about it; the anger would well up inside me. So I decided to steer clear of these conversations.

A boy I had known in high school was enrolled in the journalism school at neighbouring King's College. He came to visit me one day in my dorm room, and we chatted about our experiences at university. The conversation became lively, and during it he reached out to touch my forearm. As soon as he made contact I instinctively raised my hand and struck him. He stepped back and looked at me, a mixture of confusion and pain on his face.

"Why did you hit me?" he asked.

"I don't know" was my honest reply.

"Well, you'd better figure it out, because that's not normal behaviour." We didn't speak again.

At Thanksgiving I went home for my first visit, and I realized how much I had changed. Because I was not dependent on my parents for food and shelter anymore, I felt free to openly question and challenge their ways. I wasn't there twenty-four hours before I found myself speaking out in ways I never would have dared while still living at home.

Dad was in the basement watching a Western with one of his friends when he yelled up to my mother to bring down some fresh drinks. "Get your own goddamn drinks!" I yelled back from upstairs. I heard him bounding up the staircase in that familiar foot pattern he had when he was enraged. He came straight for me, his fist up in the air.

I was ready for him. "Go ahead, hit me, you chauvinist pig!" I had learned the phrase in my "theory of feminism" class, and Dad obviously didn't like it. His face became red, and he looked like he was about to explode. I ran out the door, down the front steps, and straight toward the white Lincoln Continental he had gotten at a bankruptcy auction. I was overcome with rage, oblivious to everything around me, as I booted in the panels with my steel-toed boots. Then I ran off into the night. I returned later, when I was sure Dad would have passed out, and packed my bag for an early departure the following morning. The next day I slipped out of town. Neither of us ever mentioned the incident again.

Partway through that first year of university, Grant broke up with me. He told me I was too dependent on him and that he wanted to be free from the confines of our relationship. I was surprised to hear this, because I'd been spending far more time with Julia than with Grant. But it was true that whenever we were together, he insisted on calling all the shots and having me as a passive sidekick. Still, I felt dead inside, and I realized I had no one in the world I could talk to. I had not made any friends besides Julia, whose response was, "That's great! Now you can sleep with lots of men instead of just one!"

Needing someone else to talk to, I made an appointment with the dean, the woman who had watched me cause nothing but trouble on our dorm floor. She invited me to go to church with her, so I agreed to join her that Sunday. It didn't work; I thought the whole thing was stupid. "God can comfort you in times of need," the dean told me as we walked back to the dorm. Privately I rolled my eyes, but I said nothing. She counselled me to call my mother, and, against my better judgment, I did. After an initial preamble, I told her the news: "Mom, Grant broke up with me." There was a three-second silence, followed by a one-word reply: "Oh." And then she proceeded to talk about things that were absolutely meaningless to me. I hung up the phone angry at what I interpreted as her indifference. After this phone call I promised myself that I would never confide in her again.

With no one to talk to, I felt lost and alone, completely cut off from any human connection. I barely ate or slept for weeks, until I realized that I didn't actually miss having Grant around. I began to feel better about the situation, so much so that when he came over a month later to ask if we could get back together again, I laughed and told him no.

It wasn't long before Grant was history. I soon met Rob, a fellow business student, and embarked on a never-ending conversation from the moment we started talking. Whereas Grant had not been very smart, Rob was my intellectual equal. He loved to discuss the abstractions I found riveting in my philosophy classes. He told me that he thought I was a gem in disguise, adding that many people would pass me by simply because they judged me for my appearance and behaviour. I was struck by how completely different Rob was from Grant, most notably with respect to sex. Until I met Rob I had no idea that it wasn't just men who could experience pleasure during intercourse. Whereas Grant had no interest in what the experience held for me, Rob made my enjoyment his priority. I felt a new dimension open up in my life and wondered how Western culture could go on and on about the sexual needs of men but say nothing about a woman's sexual fulfillment.

When I returned for my second year of university I was given a private room, presumably to make studying easier. I had chosen to major in economics after a professor commented on my natural affinity for the subject. I had always loved philosophy, and I considered economics to be the philosophy of money. As well, I recognized the power of economics to shape the lives of the world's population and wanted to make a career out of it. My ambitious long-term goal was to get an M.B.A. and my Ph.D. and then work for the International Monetary Fund or the World Bank. I chose French philosophy as my minor, and although my other classes were in English, these lectures were given in French. I was much more interested in my studies during second year as the diluted general courses of first year became more focused and streamlined.

That year when I went home for a visit, I noticed that things were sliding downhill. My mother had always collected stuff, and boxes had always been piled along the walls of our home. Papers and magazines were usually strewn all over. But on this visit it was harder to navigate through what were becoming smaller and smaller pathways between the stacks of clutter. As I picked up papers and asked my mother why she was saving them, she replied that there was a recipe she wanted to try out and an article she needed to read again. She seemed to be annoyed that I was bringing it up, so I let the conversation peter out. But a feeling of heaviness remained, as though everything were suspended in time and there was no forward movement in my parents' home or in their lives. All I could think about was my dorm room back at university, how I could lock the door and shut out the world with one movement of the latch. I realized for the first time that I had never had my own space until now, and that I cherished it.

After this trip I became even more introspective, living for the weekends when I could retreat to my room and read philosophy. I related most to existentialists like Sartre and Camus. I was drawn to their underlying theme of human freedom as responsibility, as well as the direct way in which they studied such difficult human emotions as anguish and despair. I related especially to the concept of nothingness, because it accurately reflected how I felt inside. As I neared twenty, my emotional state was shifting away from having hope for my future and more into disturbing states of mind. I wanted to know the meaning of life, because mine didn't seem to have any.

I became more reclusive with each passing month and would stockpile food from the cafeteria on Friday afternoons so as not to have to leave my room until classes on Monday. I became suspicious of others' motivations and convinced myself that spending time with most people would not add anything of value to my life. Overshadowing it all was the black wave that was always in the background threatening to engulf me.

4

SLIPSTREAM

As I neared the end of my second year, a woman who sat next to me in my economics class told me about the trip she had taken out west the preceding summer. She became animated as she described it. "The mountains are spectacular. I loved every minute of it. It was all I could do to get myself back here in time for university. If you go out there, I doubt you'll come back."

By the time the class was over, I had decided to hitchhike across the country and find work in Vancouver for the summer. I would stop off in Calgary to visit Karla and Jeff. I had seen Karla only once since she'd left home five years earlier. I was excited for the first time in a long time—I couldn't wait to get away from what I considered to be my meaningless life.

I never did make it to Vancouver. Just outside Calgary, a young guy picked me up and then spent the next hour trying to convince me to go to Jasper with him. When we reached the turnoff for the highway north to Jasper, it was not the idea of going there that became the deciding factor—it was the thought of being dropped off alone in the middle of the Trans-Canada Highway late in the evening. So off to Jasper we went.

My driver had friends who lived in staff accommodation at a hotel near one end of town. We arrived late, and after meeting his friends and having a few beers, we went to sleep on our makeshift beds.

I was the first to awaken in the morning. Deciding to go outside so I would not disturb the others, I got dressed and walked out the door. Everywhere I looked there were mountains, looming towers of limestone. It was unlike any landscape I had ever seen. I felt safe and protected in the midst of these stone fortresses, and I had a feeling that I can only describe as falling in love. One peak in particular caught my attention. It was not far south of town and had the most beautiful striated face, a glacier attached to its flank, and heavy snow on its upper reaches. This was Mount Edith Cavell, and its north face is the dominant feature seen from Jasper.

I had no idea at that time just how important mountains would become to me. All I knew was that I was totally captivated. By the time the others woke up, my plan had changed; I had decided to find work here and stay for the summer.

I applied for many jobs and got the one I wanted most: tour guide on the cruise boats at Maligne Lake. The lake was a forty-five-minute drive from town. I lived in my own cabin and ate in the staff cafeteria. The other tour guides were young like me, and after the last tours of the day we would get together in one of the cabins and party. All the money I made went toward buying booze. My co-workers didn't do any drugs except pot, which I'd given up years earlier after noticing it exacerbated my depressive tendencies.

I went into town on my days off to stock up on groceries and occasionally to call home, but as the months went by I called less frequently because I realized how terrible I felt after talking with my mother. It was as though she could make me feel worthless just by having a phone conversation with me. In the rare times I was speaking, she would put down everything I was doing, everything I was thinking; when she regained control of the conversation she would ramble on about how well Frankie was doing, or about a neighbour I had never met who had cancer. I felt like I didn't matter, like she couldn't have been less interested in anything I had to say, in anything that was going on in my life.

Summer came and went in Jasper, but I decided to stay into the autumn. I could not fathom the idea of returning to the East Coast to resume my studies. At the end of September the tour operation shut down for the winter, and I ended up going to Vancouver with Dan, the brother of the boat mechanic. I felt like I was on autopilot, with no goals or plans about anything in my life. I was also unable to process anything emotional that came up in my relationships. Because I was mostly connecting with men on a sexual level, it didn't seem to matter whether I stayed with one lover or had several. The initial stages of my sexual liaisons were infinitely more exciting than what came after, and I fell into a pattern of having brief encounters with successive partners.

Dan's parents were away for the winter, so he invited me to come and stay with him in their house in North Vancouver. We partied most nights, and during the day I would take the SeaBus into downtown Vancouver and walk the streets for hours. I particularly liked the alleys: I felt more at home in the back streets than amid the glitz of the city's main drags. I had saved up some money from the summer work, but I had to be careful about what I spent so that I could make it last. When it was raining out, which was often, I would go to libraries and art galleries.

One day I took a ferry over to Granville Island. The dark skies and wet weather of the previous three weeks were taking their toll on me, and I was feeling overwhelmed with dark emotions as the small boat pulled into its spot at the dock. These feelings, a mixture of great sadness and engulfing despair, had become my almost constant companions. My goal was just to make it from one day to the next, as I couldn't envision any future for myself.

I walked around the market, looking at the fresh vegetables in their tidy boxes and the fresh meats in their glass cases. I wondered at the seeming pointlessness of life—something I seemed to be doing a lot lately—and admitted to myself for the first time that I didn't really want to be alive. Stopping in front of a fish stall, I looked at the candied salmon through the glass. It was one of my favourite foods, but I knew it was a luxury I wasn't going to spend any of my savings on. When I looked up from the salmon, my eyes met those of the man behind the counter. His face broke into a big smile. He had a space between his two front teeth, just like I did back then, and I couldn't help but return his smile. I felt my heart lift out of its blackness, and I felt light for the first time in months.

Two days later I called Jane, and she told me she'd been in the hospital with a serious illness. She asked me if I could come home and help her out. I told her that I would fly home as soon as possible. I hadn't been home for over a year, and I decided I would fly into Saint John to visit my parents before heading to Fredericton to be with Jane. In retrospect, I'm not sure why I kept trying to reach out to them. I know that I often felt guilty for not staying in contact with them, and I had a lot of self-doubt about my interpretation of things that had happened. As well, Richard, who was still living at home, made it clear he felt I had abandoned him after letting him spend so many years glued to my side. Every time I called he would ask me when I was coming home for a visit. His was the only voice that broke through my walls and pulled on my heartstrings.

When I landed in Saint John I took a cab to my parents' place. I got out of the car, shouldered my knapsack, and walked up to the front door. As I turned the handle I heard my mother's footsteps coming toward the front door, and I was excited at the thought of her surprise at seeing me. When I opened the door, she had a big smile on her face. But the instant she saw that it was me, her expression changed.

"Oh, it's just you," she said. "I thought it was Frankie, coming home after school." And she turned around and went back into the kitchen.

I was devastated, and my black mood did not improve. I decided to stay a few days to visit with Richard, but I promised myself I would never visit my parents again.

Later that night I was lying on the couch in the living room, listening to the Massey Lectures on CBC Radio. Doris Lessing was presenting the third essay in her five-part series "Prisons We Choose to Live Inside." She was using as her launching pad apartheid South Africa, but she was talking about the human condition.

There was a coffee table in front of me, low and rectangular, on top of which I had placed my cup of tea. The radio was blaring from the adjacent dining room, and my mother was listening to this program as well, albeit from the kitchen. For some reason Lessing's words gave me strength: she was speaking about our ability to choose what we wanted in life and, more importantly, how we saw life in the first place. She talked about the prison of the psyche, where all rigid and oppressive structures and institutions came from. She talked about the group mind, and the tendency of most people to blindly follow the dictates of authority figures and social movements at the expense of their own inner knowing. I was spellbound.

Then we heard Dad's car pull into the driveway. We didn't know where he had been, but then again, we did. We knew that he went drinking with his buddies whenever he could slip out of the house, which was often. We knew that he had trouble dealing with his anger when he drank, so we were prepared to walk on eggshells and keep the peace until he went to bed and fell asleep.

Doris Lessing was talking about the spiritual element now, using words like "soul" and "god." I was curious about this, because neither of my parents had ever spoken of religion or spirituality.

At this point, Dad had taken off his shoes and was coming up the stairs into the living room. He sat down across from me, and as he heard the words coming out of the radio, he exploded. "Who in hell do these Christians think they are, spewing their doctrine of lies all around the world? They are the single greatest cause of misery for mankind, and the sooner people realize it the better!" His fists pounded the table and his face was crimson. He looked directly at me with rage in his eyes. I, as usual, was silent. "Margo, if you ever meet a Christian, run the other way as fast as you can. They will smile to your face and stab you in the back as soon as you're out of sight."

I wasn't about to bring up the fact that my father was completely missing the point. Instead, I decided to get out of there as soon as I could.

I hitchhiked to Fredericton the following day and made my way to the address Jane had given me. I walked up to a house in an older section of town and knocked on the door. A woman answered, and I asked her if Jane was home. "Margo, don't you recognize me?" the woman replied. It was Jane. But she looked much older and more tired than I had ever seen her. There were black rings around her eyes, and her skin was pale. She kept running her fingers through her hair, which she had obviously cut herself.

Jane made coffee while she recounted the events that had led up to her illness. "They told me I have mononucleosis, but basically I burned myself out." She had been going full tilt since Erin was born, two months before Jane graduated from high school, and Erin was now five. In addition to supporting herself and Erin all those years, Jane had put herself through university on a scholarship. She was one course shy of obtaining her chartered accountant designation when the stress caught up with her and she ended up in the hospital. When she was finally able to use a telephone, she called Mom and asked her if she could pick Erin up at kindergarten. But my mother refused. Jane then called Dad at work. When she told him what was happening, he grabbed his car keys and made the hour-long drive to Fredericton to pick up his granddaughter.

By now we were beyond being shocked by anything my mother did or said. We knew it wasn't normal, but we also knew that we could not speak to her about her behaviour. We had decided years before that the best way to deal with her was to just let her be, because engaging with her cold self-righteousness felt like entering a black hole that ate up our energy.

I stayed with Jane for a few months, but I wasn't much help. My depressions deepened when I was around my family, and my dark moods were hard on anyone close to me. I had begun having what I called my "mystery illness"—once or twice a month I would puke uncontrollably until I spit up blood and bile. After each episode I would feel calm for about a day, and then I would feel the tension start to build all over again. I was still drinking every day and was naïve enough not to consider this a problem. I started to see a psychologist because my lack of a will to live was scaring me. But these visits did nothing for me; I had the distinct feeling that my psychologist had only a textbook idea of what depression was. I was falling apart as the world was caving in on me, and I realized how much happier I had been when I was living in the mountains. I decided to return to Jasper.

When I arrived, I found an elderly couple in town who rented rooms in their house for one hundred dollars a month. I got a place there and worked at a gas station through the summer of 1985. When winter came I found a job at Marmot Basin, the local ski hill, and made not much money but got lots of fresh air and sunshine. It was a relatively stable time.

I was living in a party town, and when I noticed that I could not remember a day when I had not been drunk, I quit drinking on the spot. For the next three days I cried uncontrollably in my room. I had no one with whom I felt comfortable confiding this, and I had no idea what to do about it—so I resumed drinking. In the back of my mind I knew there was something wrong, but drinking was fun, and it allowed me to loosen up and socialize with my peers.

I used my savings to buy skis and a mountain bike, and before long sports became a new outlet for me. I met Gunner, co-owner of the local bike store, and we began a strong friendship that consisted of mountain biking during the day and partying at night. Gunner introduced me to other mountain bikers and got me out into the mountains I loved. He also solved the mystery of the illness I had been suffering from for over a year at this point. "You've got an ulcer," he told me when I confided my symptoms to him. "You'd better go see a doctor. They'll give you some good advice about how to deal with it."

I made an appointment, and Gunner's diagnosis was confirmed. As the doctor listed the items I was to avoid, I was making a list of my own: yes, I'll stop eating citrus fruit and onions; no, I won't give up coffee and alcohol.

On a biking trip into the Fryatt Valley I met Lyle, and in October 1986 we started dating. My lifestyle continued much the same: mountain biking or skiing during the day and partying at night. At first things went well with Lyle; then I began to notice how he kept his distance from me. This angered me, because it reminded me of my mother's response to me. Whenever my anger surfaced, Lyle would not discuss anything with me. Instead he would tell me I needed to go for a run or a bike ride, and I gave in because physical exercise did seem to dissipate the energy inside me. I didn't know what else to do with it.

Lyle had a job with Parks Canada's fly-in trail crew and encouraged me apply for the same job when spring arrived. Parks Canada trained us to use chainsaws and then flew us into remote parts of the park to do trail maintenance and build bridges. I loved the work, and I loved the fact that I was living in a tent in what I now considered to be the best place on earth. At the end of my first season I went back to working at the ski hill, continuing my lifestyle of playing and partying in this little mountain town.

The longer I was with Lyle, however, the more frequently my anger would erupt. I began to notice a pattern: these outbursts were triggered by a combination of Lyle's emotional remoteness and what I decided was his control of our relationship by determining the level of intimacy we would share. Each eruption propelled me out into the mountains for many hours until I was too tired to be enraged. But all my activity was just a panacea; my anger kept building. One night I slipped over the edge.

On the morning of January 1, 1988, I woke up with blood all over my hands. My knuckles ached. I could not remember a thing from the previous night, but I was certain there was someone who would. I got dressed without washing the blood off my hands and walked over to Lyle's place. I went up the stairs to his bedroom and found him lying on the bed. His shirt was on the floor, torn and covered in blood.

I tentatively approached the bed and lay down on top of the covers beside Lyle. He was awake and staring at the ceiling but had not looked at me once since I entered the room. He said nothing for what seemed like an eternity. Eventually I found the courage to ask him what had happened the previous night.

"You went over the edge," he said. He flipped his hand and exposed his palm. "And I couldn't stop you. You were completely out of control. All I could do was try to keep you from hurting yourself or anybody else."

That "anybody else" had been Lyle, who stood six feet four inches tall and weighed over two hundred pounds. How had he not been able to control me, at five foot five and one hundred and twenty pounds?

"What's the last thing you remember about last night?" he asked. He was looking at me as if I was someone he didn't really know, as if there was something about me he didn't understand.

"Ordering my second glass of wine at the bar," I replied. I had been experiencing blackouts like this since my early teens, but now they were happening after fewer and fewer drinks.

"Well, you'd better think about whether or not you should be drinking. And you'd better think about what would have pushed you over the edge like that." Then Lyle told me something that echoed what I had already heard from a number of men: "If you weren't such a wonderful person to wake up to in the morning, I could never put up with your drinking."

I left Lyle's place and walked back to the rooming house where I lived, went upstairs to my room, and lay down on my bed. I was unable to retrieve even a glimpse of the previous night, and it worried me that I had no recollection whatsoever of going into a wild rage. Feelings of vulnerability washed over me as I realized how many years this had been going on without my having a clue what actually happened during all those nights of blackouts. Jane had once asked me if I was drinking simply to go into a state of unconsciousness, because that's what it seemed like to others. But I hadn't analyzed it that far; I simply took it as a by-product of excessive partying.

I had decided to quit drinking the instant I woke up and saw my bloody hands, but when I told friends that I had quit drinking, nobody could believe it. I was renowned for my capacity to party, and even though I remembered none of it, apparently I was quite funny when drunk. However, I knew that my drinking was way out of control, and had been for years. I also knew that it was time to seek professional help: I was not making any headway in dealing with my bouts of depression and anger. While I could trace these feelings all the way back to childhood, I was unable to put my finger on exactly what I was so angry about. I knew my mother had neglected me and had even been cruelly cold toward me, but beyond this I had no idea why things were happening as they were or why I was in such a constant state of rage and pain.

I made an appointment with a psychologist in Hinton, a town forty-five minutes east of Jasper. I hitchhiked in early so as to be on time. I was nervous; I had no idea what to tell her. I simply thought there was *something* wrong with me.

Brenda was a gentle woman in her mid-thirties. I felt at ease with her even as she showed me into her office. There was a desk, an office chair, and a much more comfortable chair that was obviously meant for me to sit in.

"So, Margo, what seems to be the problem?" Brenda looked directly into my eyes, and the contact unnerved me.

I started talking about the recent violent episode with Lyle, but Brenda quickly turned the conversation to the topic I never discussed with anybody: my depressions.

"How long have you been experiencing these?" she asked.

"For as long as I can remember. I can't remember the last time I felt happy, not even when I was a child."

Brenda asked me if there was a pattern to my depressions, or if I noticed the episodes moving in sync with my menstrual cycles. I told her I didn't have a clue, that I had never analyzed it beyond simply trying to keep my head above water. We spent the rest of that first hour trying to track my depressions, to see if there were any patterns or if we could discern any triggers. Brenda gave me some articles to read and scheduled another appointment.

The following week I arrived at her office again, and after we had reviewed the literature she had loaned me, Brenda asked me if I ever felt suicidal.

I replied, "Well, I often feel like I don't want to be alive, if that's what you mean."

She excused herself as she picked up her phone and dialled out. After a short conversation with someone at the other end, she hung up the receiver and asked me if I would like to go down the hallway to speak to a psychiatrist who was more equipped than she was to deal with the level of depression I was experiencing.

Whatever comfort I had felt with Brenda quickly disappeared as I entered the psychiatrist's office. He was old and had stern features like a scolding father. He motioned me to sit down in the plush chair on one side of the desk and resumed his position on the other side. The only difference between his office and Brenda's was that he was sitting in an equally plush chair opposite me, and the lighting was dimmer. I wondered if this was for my benefit or his.

As soon as we were seated, he pulled some papers out of a drawer and began to take notes. He asked me a series of questions, and I felt more like a subject in a lab than a real human being sitting across from him. As soon as I answered one question he would fire the next one at me. I could tell that he was not making them up on the fly, that this was some sort of test, or at least a predetermined line of thought.

Finally he was out of questions. He leaned back in his chair and made a pronouncement that would alter the way I looked at myself for the next two decades.

"You exhibit all the symptoms of a manic-depressive. There is only one cure for this disorder, and that is to go on antidepressant drugs, which I can prescribe for you. I would put you on lithium. We've had a lot of success with this in cases such as yours."

I asked the only question that came into my mind: "How long would I need to be on them?"

Without a moment's hesitation the psychiatrist said, "For the rest of your life. There's a chance that you could get better eventually, but it usually doesn't get any better with age. In fact, it can get a lot worse."

I couldn't imagine worse. I had read about people who were manic-depressive. They were labelled "mentally ill," and although it was one thing to be considered to have a mental illness, it was altogether different to be on drugs to treat it. As he wrote out the prescription, I felt like I was already on the drugs. I could not believe what was happening to me and what it would all mean.

I walked out of his office, back onto the streets, and when I reached the highway I stuck out my thumb and caught a ride to Jasper. An elderly couple stopped to pick me up, and as I sat in the back seat I kept thinking, "What would these people think if they knew I had a mental illness, that I needed to go on prescription drugs for the rest of my life?"

I never did fill that prescription. By the time I got back to Jasper I had decided that I was going to heal myself or kill myself, but I was not going on pharmaceutical drugs for the rest of my life. I concluded that the psychiatrist was full of shit; he could not possibly know in one sitting what I was all about, especially when he hadn't even tried to find out anything about my past. I knew even then that there were reasons for my behaviour, reasons that extended all the way back to my childhood. And although the details of its origins eluded me, I knew my problem was not a chemical imbalance and that the drugs I was being offered would only obscure the truth about my mental instability.

But the decisive factor was the feeling in the pit of my stomach that I was in danger and should run away from these professionals as fast as I could. My childhood had left me with a deep distrust of authority figures, and I had instinctively lumped the psychiatrist in with parents, teachers, cops, and clergy.

Although I chose not to take the psychiatrist's drugs, I did accept his diagnosis: I now knew that I, like my mother and grandmother before me, suffered from serious bouts of depression. The burning question was how to deal with these bouts so I did not end up like them.

Two months later I received a parcel from Jane that contained a paper-back book, *The Nature of Personal Reality* by Jane Roberts. It was unlike any book I had ever read, making sense of the world in a way that mainstream culture did not. In a section on depression, Roberts maintained that individuals were at all times in control of their state of mind; if that state was negative or destructive, it was only because the individual's underlying belief system supported this mode of thinking. The author went further, asserting that individuals chose their particular illnesses, whether physical or mental, for a reason: as a constructive challenge that could lead to that person's greater fulfillment. In other words, every mental or physical symptom contained within it the seeds of its own healing.

I reread the section several times, wondering if this could possibly be true. Could I be the source of my own depression? I was fascinated by the concept, not least because it put the power of reshaping my psyche into my hands. I felt validated for trusting my own instinct and not opting for lithium. I decided this would be my experiment: to see if I could alter the landscape of my psyche using elements of my belief system as the underlying building blocks.

The first step, quitting drinking, turned out to be harder than I had imagined. I soon found out that not ingesting alcohol was only a small part of giving up the habit. Because the temptation was so huge for me, I could not go anywhere where alcohol was served, or hang out with anyone who drank. My relationship with Lyle petered out over the next few months, and the rest of my social life dried up too. I did, however, begin to hang around with a woman I had met the previous summer. I had always thought of Tara as too straight for my liking, but now that I was sober I realized we had much more in common than I had originally thought—we were interested in a lot of the same things and were both trying to sort through the complexities of our childhoods. We started meeting often, usually at her place, to drink herbal tea and discuss everything under the sun. The only other female with whom I'd had intimate conversations was Sarah, my long-ago friend from the Village Mart. And because Tara and I were both adults, we were able to relate on a completely different level. It was a relief to find her, and the timing could not have been more perfect.

By the time my second season of trail crew began in the spring of 1988, I had been sober for five months and was not doing drugs. I had always been able to take or leave drugs as long as I had my substance of choice (alcohol) for self-medication. But I began to wonder how I would feel when the guys were drinking beer during the evenings after work. I had been promoted to lead hand this year, and I got lucky: it turned out that the guys on my crew were not big drinkers, so I did not feel out of place after all.

The work was fun and engaging, and the projects were varied. We flew in to some of the most remote reaches of Jasper's north and south boundary trail systems. Sometimes we were tasked to clear the flora from the sides of the trails, and at other times we built bridges over creeks and rivers. All we had for tools were chainsaws, sledgehammers, and spikes, and we used local trees for wood on construction projects. Although I have to admit that I was not the most decisive leader, I managed to accomplish all of my tasks on each trip and became increasingly confident in my abilities with each assignment.

I was twenty-four years old and feeling better than I ever had. And then I met Jay.

5

MEXICAN OVERDRIVE

I CAN STILL REMEMBER THE FIRST TIME I laid eyes on him. It was a cool evening in June, and Tara and I had driven out to Jasper's Tekarra Lodge to have a quiet dinner. No sooner had we walked through the door than some people she knew invited us to join them at their table. I recognized some of the people seated there; those I didn't know turned out to be building contractors from Jasper and Whistler, British Columbia. Among them was a striking man who looked to be in his mid-thirties.

Jay was tall and slim, with curly blond hair that barely reached his neck. His eyes were an incredible shade of blue, and the contrast between his tanned skin and his blue eyes made them stand out even more. He was dressed in jeans and a faded flannelette shirt and had an air of certainty about him, a confidence that I had rarely seen in another human being. He was powerfully charismatic, and over the next two hours he enchanted everyone with his intelligence and wit. I stayed on the sidelines, watching things unfold, mesmerized by this figure at the centre of it all. I had never seen anyone so dominate a social setting, and I had never felt such an intense connection with another person.

Jay and I kept running into each other after this first meeting: at the post office, in the grocery store. We made small talk, but it was obvious to both of us that there was a mutual attraction. Two weeks after our initial meeting, he walked over to me in the middle of a busy café. It was the first time we had spoken privately, and I felt completely at ease. We talked about people we knew in common, where we worked, and what our schedules were like. We laughed a lot—Jay had a wicked sense of humour. Then his eyes softened and he said, "Let's go for a drive in my truck."

We drove up to an isolated lake, where Jay led me down a short trail to a private clearing. When we stopped, he took my hands in his and gazed into my eyes.

"I have a wife, and a daughter," he began. "We're not in love. It's a marriage of convenience. I can't stop thinking about you, and I'm struggling with my overwhelming feelings for you. What do you think we should do?"

"We should sleep together" was my instant reply. And I meant it; at the age of twenty-four I believed the intensity of my feelings was a measure of their rightness.

Jay and I had to be cautious because we were living in a small town. Initially we set up meetings through a mutual friend, until one day Jay told me that I could get him a second key to my mailbox at the post office and we could communicate by leaving notes there for each other. He said that he and his wife had an arrangement—they were together for the sake of their child, but if either of them met someone else, they would go their separate ways. I asked him when he was going to tell her about me, and he replied that he had to wait until the time was right. I wanted to ask him more about this but decided that because he knew the situation better than I did, I would leave it alone.

Jay didn't like phones and refused to use them for any of our communications. We continued our relationship in this clandestine way—leaving notes for each other, and meeting up whenever we could—for two months. In late August, he made me an offer I couldn't refuse.

"I'm leaving for Whistler in a few days," he told me as we were driving back from a tryst. "I've got a contract to build houses there for the winter, and I've got some other work to do. I'll buy you a one-way train ticket to Vancouver that leaves the day after you finish work. Once you arrive, I'll fill you in on the details of our new life together."

I had never been in love like this, and I felt I was entering a dream world, an exotic new planet where I had love in my heart and secret adventure in my soul. Although we had no further communication, Jay was in Vancouver to pick me up at the train station when I arrived in mid-September.

We sped from the station to a hairstyling studio where he had already booked an appointment for me. Apparently my current look was a little too "wild." "Your carefree style might go over well in Jasper," Jay told me, "but if you're going to accompany me on business trips and to upscale restaurants, you're going to need a makeover." Straight after this we went clothes shopping, and Jay picked out and paid for the first formal clothing I had ever owned. By the end of the afternoon I looked like any other well-adjusted young woman out on the town with her lover.

Jay and I had never had the luxury of spending any length of time together while we were carrying on our affair in Jasper. But on my first night in Vancouver, over dinner in an expensive Italian restaurant, Jay explained that while he would be overseeing construction projects in Whistler, he also had other business interests in several cities in the United States.

"You don't need to bother yourself with any of the details, but I'll need to go down to the States on a pretty regular basis. Most of the time we'll drive, but occasionally we'll fly. We'll be meeting with some pretty high-powered business contacts of mine. You'll have fun. You'll meet lots of interesting people and eat at some of the best restaurants in North America."

As I picked at my seafood appetizer, it dawned on me that I had moved out to the coast to be with a man I barely knew. I asked Jay the first question that popped into my mind. "What kind of business are you involved in?"

Jay took a drink of his wine and allowed a broad smile to cross his face before he replied. "It's better if you don't know too many details at this point. The business I'm in is very competitive, and we're trying to bring something new to the market. All of us have promised to keep it a secret until we're ready to unveil." Jay went on to explain that this part of our life, not just our affair, had to be kept secret. He also told me that while we were travelling and meeting with his business associates, he got to call all the shots.

As far as I was concerned, Jay was already calling all the shots. Because our affair had to be kept secret from his family, and because he had obligations to his wife and daughter, he was the one who decided when we spent time together, and for how long. I'd had no way of contacting him directly when we were in Jasper, and I consoled myself with the fact that I now got to spend huge amounts of time with him out on the coast. He repeatedly told me that we would be together legitimately when the timing was right, that I just had to be patient. I believed him, because in those first few months I had no reason not to.

He had already set up my life in Whistler in the form of a job on the construction site he was overseeing. He had also set up our home base, a semi-detached condo in a well-established neighbourhood. "You can show up for work whenever you like," he told me as we drove to Whistler on that first night. "Our main priority will be the business trips, but I figured a bit of work would keep you from getting bored."

I had never been to Whistler, and even though it was late when we drove into town, I knew immediately I was going to love it there. The town was nestled in the Coast Mountains, at an elevation where it stayed cooler year-round than the rest of the Lower Mainland. There was a big ski hill and lots of tanned, fit, and healthy people. In many ways it was just like Jasper.

We pulled into the driveway of the condo, and Jay pushed the button on the automatic garage door opener. As soon as we were parked he closed the door again. We grabbed my luggage—one backpack and one suitcase—out of the back of the truck and brought them inside. I loved our new home the moment I stepped foot in the door. It was unlike any place I had ever lived in, a two-level condo, with kitchen, living, and dining room on the main floor, and two bedrooms on the second floor. There was a fireplace in the master bedroom, as well as the largest bathroom I had ever seen. The furniture was sparse, but functional and tasteful.

We wasted no time getting to bed. It had been a big day for me, not just because of the travelling, but also because of the volume of information I had absorbed about the new life I was embarking on.

Jay and I quickly established our routine in Whistler. We would leave for the job site together in the morning and cut out early every afternoon. Back at home, Jay would disappear into the second bedroom, which he used as an office, and do paperwork and make phone calls, while I went for a run on one of the many trails in our neighbourhood. Evenings, we'd go out for dinner. Jay didn't like to cook, and he felt that it wasn't necessary given the volume of restaurants in the area. "We've got more money than time," he told me. "Besides, it's a great way to end our days. We can focus on the business end of things and let the food professionals focus on theirs."

During our first month in Whistler, Jay introduced me to cocaine. I had tried it before, but as he cut up our first lines on a flat piece of stone that he obviously kept for this purpose, Jay assured me, "You've never had anything like the stuff I'm about to give you. This is uncut, straight off the plane from Colombia." When the lines were ready, he took a short straw and proceeded to do the larger of the two lines. Then he handed me the straw so I could do mine.

It soon became obvious to me that Jay was a full-blown addict. About once a month he would receive a shipment of yellowish-grey granules of the finest cocaine, bound together in a fist-sized chunk with acetone. As each shipment arrived, he broke it apart into smaller chunks with a knife, then meticulously turned it back into fine powder, using a razor blade on a hard, smooth surface like a mirror or polished stone. Once it got to this stage, Jay would package the drug, in one- or two-gram portions, in folded pieces of magazine paper, which he stored in a cool, dry place. He might give some of the cocaine to an associate as a personal favour, but mostly it was for his own use.

Although I wasn't present to witness every instance, I came to the conclusion that Jay used between one and two grams of the white powder every day. Snorting coke is an easy habit to slip into. Unlike alcohol, it does not smell, and people cannot tell that you are using it. Instead of depressing the nervous system and making you sleepy, it energizes users. It is also a great mood enhancer, as it inhibits the reuptake of serotonin in the brain, causing the user to feel an expanded sense of euphoria. For someone like me, with a history of depression, it was the drug of choice from the moment I first tried it. Now it was not only plentiful, but also pure as the driven snow.

One afternoon Jay called me up to the bedroom. When I got there, he ushered me into the bathroom, where he proceeded to reach under the sink and pull out a pencil case. He unzipped it and showed me its contents. "There's ten thousand dollars cash in here. I want you to know where it is in case you ever need it."

"What would I ever need that amount of money for?" I asked him.

"You can never know why you might need it," he replied, "and that is precisely why I keep it around."

Jay handed me the canvas bag so I could replace it myself and know exactly where to find it. Later that afternoon he told me to get dressed in my new clothes. "We're going into the city for dinner. You'll be meeting two of my business partners from the States. Don't worry if you don't understand any of our business conversations. We're used to speaking in code for fear our ideas will get hijacked. Just have fun, they're great guys. And don't be offended if there's not much small talk going on. We try not to get personal in our line of work."

Two hours later we were in downtown Vancouver, in a restaurant even more upscale than the one Jay had taken me to my first night on the coast. We were escorted to our table, where two Latino men were already seated. They were both handsome and very well dressed. I realized why Jay had insisted that I style my hair and buy myself some nice clothes.

The two men spoke flawless English, albeit with an accent. After the initial introduction, the conversation turned to topics I had only read about in newspapers and magazines. The discussion of recent political developments in North and South America was so far above my head I couldn't make heads or tails of it, let alone participate, but I was fascinated; I had never met anyone with this level of comprehension about world events. I began to notice a thread in the conversation: no matter what particular topic the three men became embroiled in, they always related it back to what it would all mean in terms of government regulations and the free movement of capital around the world. I made a mental note to read more about these topics, and to pay more attention when I did.

As we drove back to Whistler that night I was still replaying parts of the dinner conversation, trying to understand some of the references, when Jay broke into my reverie. "That was great. I could tell they liked you, and that's a good sign. It's all about trust in our business. Did you see their gold jewellery?" Jay had told me that his associates loved precious metals, especially gold. "We'll bring them a gold coin next time. I like to do that every now and then as a token of appreciation for our partnership. Most people in our line of business collect precious metals, and we mostly hide it in the ground. Did you know that in 1933 the American government confiscated gold? There's one thing you'll learn hanging around me and my colleagues: you can't trust institutions. They're basically legal cartels, and they'll do anything to keep themselves alive."

He reached into his jacket pocket and handed me a packet of coke, saying, "There's a mirror in the glove compartment. Use your credit card. There's no razor blade."

I poured a small amount of the fine powder onto the mirror, which I held flat between my knees, and formed two lines with my credit card. It took all my dexterity to carve out lines while we were driving—a skill I would master in the following months.

"This sucks," I said. "I don't have nearly the precision I do with a razor blade."

Jay explained that when we were travelling we could not afford to have any drug paraphernalia in the truck with us. Cops were trained in what to look for, and a razor blade or small straw would be a dead giveaway if the vehicle were searched. "It's not perfect, but a credit card and a rolled-up dollar bill are great stand-ins while we're on the road."

When the lines were ready, I rolled up a dollar bill and snorted my line. Then I handed the rolled-up bill to Jay as I held the mirror up where he could access it. I had made his line bigger than mine: my body was not as accustomed to the drug as his was.

The following evening we went over to his foreman's house for dinner. Tony was technically my boss, but he knew that Jay and I decided when I would show up for work. He was single, and I assumed it was because he was so dedicated to his work. Jay and Tony went over the blueprints for the next phase of the development, while I perused the bookshelves that lined the walls of Tony's study.

"Have you read Chomsky's latest book?" he asked when he saw me lingering near his bookcases.

I replied that I hadn't, all the time wondering who "Chomsky" was. (Despite my wide reading, I had no idea that Noam Chomsky was—and remains—a respected political philosopher and activist.)

As Tony and I chatted about our favourite authors, Jay reached into his pocket and pulled out the packet of coke that I was beginning to realize he always carried with him. Tony opened a drawer and handed him a mirror and a razor blade. I watched as Jay went through what was becoming a familiar procedure. He dumped a small pile of the drug onto the surface of the mirror, took the razor blade, and cut through the pile at one angle and then the opposite angle, making sure the powder was chopped up as finely as possible. He then split the pile into three equal parts and proceeded to run each pile out until it formed a long straight line. Reaching into his pocket to take out a dollar bill, he rolled it up tightly until it formed a paper straw. Then he motioned for Tony to go first.

Tony took the straw and leaned over the mirror. He put the straw up to his right nostril, used his left index finger to plug his left nostril, and then ran the makeshift straw up the line of cocaine as he inhaled deeply. I took the straw from his outstretched hand and did my line, and then Jay did his. Jay left the packet and the bill on the mirror and put everything back in the drawer that Tony had taken it out of.

One week later, Jay informed me that we would be driving to Portland the following day. He told me exactly what to pack for the trip. "You'll be meeting more people, and you'll like them just as much as you did my other two partners. I may need to take off at some point to look after some critical business, but we'll be staying in a five-star hotel, so you won't feel stranded. Mostly we'll just be having fun."

Nothing could have been further from the truth. These trips were often tense and stressful for Jay. Whenever I asked him about this, which was often, he told me that he had a lot of money riding on the success of his ventures, and that meeting with the key players in these ventures brought him face to face with the risks involved. I tried to press him for more information, but he refused to discuss it with me.

"You don't understand," he would say. "And I'm not at liberty to go around talking about the details. The best thing you can do for me is to stop asking me about the business and just focus on the relaxing and fun parts of these trips. Just treat them like mini-vacations."

We arrived in Portland mid-afternoon the following day and checked in to the most beautiful hotel I had ever seen, let alone stayed in. Once Jay and I were settled in the room, he explained that he had to go out for a couple of hours. I could just relax in the room or go down to the spa. "I'll be back around six, and we'll have dinner together down in the lobby. They've got a great restaurant here."

He returned two hours later in a great mood. I interpreted this to mean he had been successful in whatever he had gone out to do. Over dinner that night he told me that we would be driving home the following day, making one quick stop along the way.

The following morning we drove straight to Bellingham, Washington, a city about fifty miles south of Vancouver. As we pulled into the driveway of a private home, I saw an attractive man in his mid-thirties get up from a lawn chair and walk toward the double garage that Jay was driving into. When we were inside, the automatic door closed behind us. We got out of the truck, and Jay introduced me to Greg before we went into the house.

Greg had a light lunch prepared for us—cheese, crackers, and olives. We picked a few bits off the plate as we chatted, and I was surprised to find that he and Jay were talking about politics and not whatever business Jay had come here to do. After about twenty minutes, Greg took me into the backyard where I could wander around the garden while he and Jay took care of their business in the garage. Ten minutes later, Jay and I were back in the truck, heading for the border. Jay told me that Greg would be coming up to our place that evening to finish off their business dealings.

When Greg arrived, he drove straight into our garage, and Jay closed the door behind him. Jay told me to prepare some snacks while he and Greg were out in the garage. But the next thing I knew, they were back in the house and Greg was telling us that he needed to get back home as soon as possible.

After a few weeks in Whistler I began to notice what I can only refer to as paranoid tendencies in Jay. A month and a half into our new life, these escalated to a whole new level. Jay had been especially tense for a few days, and as usual he refused to discuss it with me. Late one night we were lying awake on the bed; we had done too much coke to go to sleep at our regular hour. For the first time, Jay started talking about the details of his situation.

"There's this guy, he used to be in the business, but he had to take a break. Now he wants back in, and I'm afraid he's going to try to push me out."

I asked Jay how this man could possibly push him out.

"He's still got powerful connections, and once you've been in at his level, it's pretty hard to get pushed back out."

Then Jay did something that shocked me: he went into the closet and came out with a handgun.

"I'm sorry to spring it on you like this, but there are firearms in the house, and right now I can't sleep unless I've got one under my pillow."

I was astounded. Other than my father's hunting rifles, I had never been around guns. And yet I wasn't scared. The news had been introduced so abruptly and come so far out of left field that I couldn't take it in enough to feel any emotional response. I lay awake for hours, wondering just what type of business Jay was involved in where you needed guns to protect yourself. I also wondered if this fear was the result of his cocaine use; I had heard that people became paranoid after using the drug for prolonged periods. Eventually I fell asleep. Jay slept with his handgun for three nights in a row, but after that he never mentioned the incident, or his fears, again.

6

REALITY BATH

LESS THAN A MONTH AFTER OUR TRIP to Portland, we headed south again. This time we flew to San Francisco.

"Why do we keep meeting people in different cities?" I asked Jay as we drove to the airport.

"Because we're all from different parts of the continent, and we can meet anywhere," he told me. "San Francisco is beautiful. You'll be happy we're meeting there once you see the place."

We took a taxi straight from the airport in San Francisco to a restaurant downtown. Once again we were led to a table where two Latino men were seated. I was briefly introduced, and then Jay looked over the wine list and ordered one of the most expensive bottles of red on the menu. I was two years into my sobriety and not tempted to partake in any drinking. Besides, the effects of cocaine were coursing through my veins. Although I had no idea how he managed to do it, Jay always seemed to have a packet of coke in his pocket. Glasses clinked, appetizers arrived at the table, and the men got down to business.

The dinner conversation was riveting, as usual, and now I had a better understanding of what they were talking about. I was reading more about current affairs and drawing on my studies of economics at university. Although Jay and his associates had a different take on what was happening than any view I had heard from anyone else, I noticed that there were no inconsistencies with the facts I had learned in my studies. I felt like I was getting a tutorial on how things really worked in the world, as opposed to how we were told they worked, and I found it fascinating.

Halfway through the meal, the conversation turned to the "War on Drugs." One of Jay's associates said that the Drug Enforcement Agency had set up roadblocks on highways about a third of the way up the states of California and Texas to catch illegal Mexican immigrants travelling north. The men discussed how this would affect the movement of black market products. It became obvious that my dinner companions believed the "War on Drugs" was just a front for the more nefarious activities of the U.S. government, and that it had more to do with controlling the movement of capital than with caring about kids in ghettos getting hooked on drugs. They talked about how prisons were being privatized and becoming a lucrative business, and they argued that drug charges were proving to be one of the fastest and easiest ways to fill these institutions with marginalized people.

Jay's associates spoke with authority about the Mexican and Colombian drug cartels' awareness that the United States was exploiting their countries, using corporations and the government's foreign policy as carried out by agencies like the World Bank and the International Monetary Fund. I got the sense that the drug cartels in these countries shared the key goal of forming their own South American banking system so they could free themselves from Wall Street banks.

This conversation picked up where my formal education in economics classes at university had left off and filled me in on the other half of the equation: the black market world of beneath-the-surface money and power. My childhood had ensured that I lost all respect for the institutions in our culture, and my rebellious nature set me up perfectly to embrace the ideology in which I was now immersed.

When the second bottle of wine was getting low, Jay ordered a bottle of Dom Perignon. I had the distinct feeling that it was a night of celebration for everyone around the table, but I was not privy to exactly what was being celebrated. Finally the cocaine wore off and the bottles were drained. Jay and I took a taxi to our hotel and fell asleep in our exhaustion.

The next day, Jay left me at the hotel for a few hours while he looked after his business. We caught a flight back to Vancouver later that afternoon.

During our time in Whistler, it was not unusual for Jay to be gone for a few days during any given week. He explained that he needed to attend to more business matters, and that there was no need for me to come along on all of his trips. He also revealed that some of these trips took him back to Alberta, where he would be stopping in to see his family before returning to Whistler. Each time he mentioned his wife and daughter, I became uncomfortable. I literally forgot about them during the intense time that Jay and I spent together, and then their reality would come crashing into my psyche when Jay brought them up. I felt like I was being held captive: I wasn't allowed to tell anyone where I was living or what I was doing because Jay feared this could lead to his wife finding out about us. I couldn't even answer the phone. It was as if I were a ghost, cut off from everything that was not directly related to Jay and his business dealings.

During the third week of November we were heading south on another business trip, this time to Los Angeles. We left after work on Thursday, and Jay drove through to L.A. in one push because he didn't like to let me drive. I ended up getting some sleep during the night, but by the time we arrived at our hotel on Friday, he hadn't slept a wink. It was warm and sunny, and Jay encouraged me to go out to the pool for a swim and some sun tanning. He said he'd come down to join me once he had taken care of some business.

Around five in the afternoon we went up to the room to get changed, then walked through the lobby to the restaurant. I loved the weather in L.A., so balmy compared with the socked-in clouds and rain of Vancouver. We were the only patrons in the restaurant, which suited us just fine—we were exhausted.

As we ate, Jay explained that a complication had arisen. "I'm having a bit of a problem getting in touch with my contacts here," he told me. "We may need to stay for an extra day or two. It's not ideal, but we have no choice."

The next twenty-four hours were stressful. Jay couldn't leave the hotel room for fear he would miss a phone call. I alternated between hanging out in the room with Jay and going down to the pool, picking up snacks and bottled water from the restaurant on my way back to the room. We watched TV and did the odd line of cocaine. I fell asleep later that night, but Jay only managed to doze lightly, for brief periods. The following day was much the same, but this time I stayed awake and Jay drifted off occasionally. He told me not to fall asleep while he was napping; if I needed to rest or go out for snacks, I should wake him to ensure we did not miss a phone call.

At six that evening the phone rang. Jay's contacts said they would meet him in the hotel parking lot in half an hour. We packed our stuff, and he told me to go to the front desk and check out while he went to meet with his colleagues.

As I exited the hotel and walked toward the truck, I saw Jay and two men putting what looked like duffel bags into the back. They shook hands, and the two men left before I got to the vehicle. We drove off immediately, heading back out to the I-5. Jay knew of a small town about two hours away where we could get a room and some much-needed sleep. He was exhausted. Dark rings circled his eyes, and his skin was ashen. His relief was palpable as we navigated the traffic out of the city. I couldn't stop wondering what was in the duffel bags, but considering the state Jay was in, I decided to wait until he got some rest before I questioned him.

The next day we started driving around noon and made it to Greg's place the following morning. This time there was no conversation. Jay and Greg simply left me in the house while they attended to their business in the garage. As soon as they were done, we left. We were two days later than we had anticipated and too burned out to socialize.

The following evening I was alone in the condo, aware that Greg would be arriving at any moment. Jay usually made a point of being home when any of his associates came by, but he'd had to go out of town to collect some money. When I heard the sound of a vehicle in the driveway and saw Greg's truck through the small window in the front door, I went to the garage and pushed the button to open the automatic door. Greg drove straight in and I closed the door behind him.

As soon as we had greeted each other, I went back into the house and left Greg to finish up his business. A few minutes later he came inside and we made a bit of small talk—yes, the traffic was light; no, he would not be staying over but would make the trip home that night.

Then he asked, "Where's Jay?"

"He's away on business," I replied.

"Well, I need to talk to him. I'm not happy with our current business arrangement. I'm not making enough money."

"You'll have to take that up with him yourself," I replied calmly, though I was suddenly keenly aware that I was alone in the house with a man I barely knew.

Greg did not say any more about the arrangement, and I wished him a safe drive home as I hit the button on the garage door.

When Jay returned the following day, I told him about my conversation with Greg. He was livid.

"He knows better than that!" he yelled. "It's me he's supposed to be dealing with. He is totally out of line bringing that up with you."

I felt uncomfortable about the interaction with Greg, and Jay's response only confirmed my feelings and left me wondering what exactly was going on in the garage and with those duffel bags in Los Angeles. I began to question who Jay was and what the fuck I was doing with my life. Should I just pack up and leave? I wondered. But where would I go? And what would I be going back to? It was becoming increasingly clear to me that I had not really had a life before Jay.

I went back upstairs and did another line of coke.

We were moving into the latter part of December, and while the weather was overcast and rainy on the coast, it was crisp and cold when we returned to Jasper for Christmas.

I was glad to be back in town, cross-country skiing during the day and visiting my old friend Tara every evening. My life on the coast seemed like a dream; the only part that seemed real was my bond with Jay. But I could not ignore the fact that I was the odd person out. Here I was, during a holiday that was supposed to be spent relaxing with those closest to me, alone in my room while Jay was with his wife and daughter. I felt discarded—I mattered when it came to accompanying him on his business trips, but not when it came to my feelings about his going back to his family and pretending to be the husband and father. At times I couldn't help asking myself if *that* was his real life, and if he was merely pretending to be my partner. But whenever I expressed my doubts to Jay, he would assure me that I was his real connection and that his wife and daughter were just the props he used to project the stable image of a family man to the world.

I couldn't understand why he was stalling and not telling Liz that he was in love with me. There was nothing I could do about it, however, so I resorted to enjoying the beauty of the mountains and going out in the snow every day to exercise. Soon I was packing to leave again, and early one morning Jay and I headed out of town.

We got as far as Mount Robson before I could no longer contain myself. "So, did you tell Liz about us?"

There was a moment of silence before Jay answered. "Of course not. It's Christmas, for God's sake. Who brings up something like that over the holidays?"

"Well, when are you going to tell her?"

Jay became tense, as he always did when I brought up the issue, but his voice stayed calm. "I'll tell her when the time is right. In the meantime, I need you to stop forcing my hand."

I dropped the subject.

Two weeks later, Jay told me he needed me to go inland without him. He spent the day outlining everything I would need to do. The following afternoon I boarded a plane to Edmonton, where I took a taxi to a downtown hotel. When I arrived, I called the phone number Jay had given me. Twenty minutes later a car pulled up in front of my hotel, and the driver motioned to me with a hand signal. I got in and he pulled back out into the traffic. I had a box with me, wrapped in brown paper, and I put it in the foot well of the car. The driver placed a brown envelope on the seat between us, which I promptly put in my shoulder bag. Within minutes, he pulled up in front of the hotel again, and I got out and went back up to my room. The next morning I caught a taxi to the airport and boarded a plane to Vancouver.

When Jay picked me up, we drove straight to a car dealership. While I was away, he had decided we needed another vehicle. Not only was his large truck impractical for driving the long distances down to the States, but we also needed something for me to take on the road when I had to travel on my own.

We quickly chose the car we wanted—a blue Acura Legend—and took it for a test drive. By the time we returned to the dealership, we knew we were going to buy it. We went into the salesman's office, where Jay opened up his briefcase and counted out the money—$30,000 in cash. I registered the astonished look on the salesman's face, even as he tried to hide his shock.

Jay and I drove home in our separate vehicles, and I marvelled at how well the new car handled on the Sea to Sky Highway. But by the time I got back to the condo, I was ready to confront Jay about his behaviour and my suspicions.

"Do you think I'm stupid?" I asked once we were inside our condo. "Didn't you see the look on the salesman's face when you showed him all that cash? He could be calling the cops right now, reporting our purchase as an unusual transaction."

Jay looked at me defiantly. "And what do you suggest I should have done? Would you rather I take out a loan on the vehicle and make us go through the song and dance of all that paperwork? That salesman doesn't care how we paid for that car. All he cares about is his commission. Forget about it. You've just got to trust me, I know what's going on and you don't."

"Exactly my point, Jay. You want me to blindly follow you around, from business meeting to dinner engagement, and say nothing and ask no questions. Don't you think I know what you're doing? What the hell did you get me to take to Edmonton for you? I felt like a sitting duck on that plane. If you want me to continue with this, you're going to have to level with me."

"You don't understand, Margo. It's better if you don't know what's going on. It will protect you if anything happens. And you've got the car now. You never have to feel like a sitting duck again."

I got changed to go for a run. "I'll be back in an hour. I need to clear my head."

Jay hugged me as I turned to leave. "We'll go out for a nice dinner tonight and I'll answer as many of your questions as I can. Just hang in there. I promise everything will be okay."

At dinner, Jay told me everything. He was involved with Mexican and South American drug cartels. They were moving product north through their chain of connections and using these same chains to take the money back down south. Everyone was making money during the process, but there was also an overriding goal. Jay explained how the black market economy, South American politics, and power struggles for control of the region all tied into this objective, concluding: "Believe it or not, the world runs on black market money. It acts like steroids for the international financial system. All the big players know this, from the multinational corporations to the biggest officials in government. It's a huge game, and despite how stable the world might seem to you, it could all actually come tumbling down at any time. It's a veritable house of cards."

I had stopped eating and was staring at him. The conversations he'd had with his colleagues floated back to me, and I felt I finally had enough pieces to understand the puzzle.

"There's a plan," Jay continued, "and we're getting close, and by close I mean ten to twenty years out. At that point the drug cartels will have amassed enough money to go legit in a big way. That's all I can tell you for now, except that having you go to the States with me has been an enormous help. Everything had been running smoothly except border crossings. You have no idea how difficult it is to cross the border as a single male. It's one of the things the guards are trained to look out for. When you're in the car with me, I don't stand out. We're just another couple going down to the States for a wedding or on a shopping trip."

As I listened to Jay, it dawned on me that I had been recruited for a position and unwittingly placed in danger, potentially a target of the customs agents and of Jay's "associates." I needed some time to absorb everything he told me that night, but I quickly decided that I was not interested in risking my freedom for Jay; I vowed not to accompany him over the border again.

Toward the end of January, Jay told me he had to go down to the States again, this time to San Diego.

"I'm not going with you," I told him. "But if you see anyone I've already met, tell them I said hello."

I was worried that Jay might try to pressure me into going, but he didn't. He drove to San Diego alone in the new car. Two days later he was back in Whistler.

Although I refused to go to the States with him again, I did start going along on trips to other parts of British Columbia and Alberta. This seemed like the only chance I had to spend time with him when he wasn't completely preoccupied with his business.

My decision not to go to the States caused a rift in our relationship, albeit a passive one. Jay seemed more introspective, and he refused to talk about our relationship when I brought it up. I reacted to this emotional remoteness the same way I had done with Lyle. Whenever we were in Whistler, I would go for long runs in an attempt to burn off my anger at what he had gotten me involved in as well as my resentment at his refusal to tell me where I stood with him. What had once been pure, unadulterated love for Jay was now tinged with my fears and suspicions. These usually stayed below the surface of our everyday reality, but as we moved further into the new year they began to erupt more frequently.

In mid-February, we returned home after a trip to Alberta. I was unpacking my suitcase in the bedroom, and Jay had just stepped out of the shower, when the phone rang. In a state of defiance, I walked over to pick it up, but Jay intercepted me. Tony was on the line. Jay told him he was busy but that he would be over to the job site as soon as he could make it.

Jay and I stared at each other as he spoke, and we continued staring after he put the receiver back on the hook.

Finally he broke the silence. "What are you doing? What were you thinking, picking up the phone like that? It could have been Liz."

"Fuck Liz!" I yelled back. "Fuck you and your bullshit life of lies and your stupid little bitch back in Jasper. I don't give a fuck if she finds out about us. This isn't just about her or you or the business. It's also about me! When do I matter? When do I get what I want?"

Jay kept staring at me, and there was a fleeting moment when I felt that he was unsure how to proceed.

"Look at you," he finally said. "Look how out of control you are. You're a loose cannon. I can't have my life come unhinged because of you. Liz is my anchor, something you will never be. And if there's one thing I need in my line of work, it's being seen as a stable family man."

My anger was fired up to a new level by this admission. "You promised me! You told me you didn't love her and that you were only with her out of convenience. The only reason you won't leave her is because I refuse to follow you around like a puppy dog. She'll never stand up to you, and that's what you really want in a woman."

I had no idea where this was heading or what I was going to do about it. So I did what I always did when I got emotionally upset and felt my anger rushing out of control: I went for another long run in the mountains. When I returned, Jay was waiting for me so we could go out to dinner and talk things over. He explained that he was under a lot of pressure from his business colleagues but that everything was going to work out fine between us. I just had to be patient and wait.

After this I began working more on the job site with Tony. I still loved Jay but felt that I needed something to ground me that was outside his direct sphere of influence. Jay continued to make his monthly trips to the United States and his shorter trips inland during the week. Whenever he was home, we would go out to a different restaurant every night, where we continued to have fascinating conversations about international politics and finance.

In March 1989 we were staying in Vancouver at a favourite hotel on Davie Street. We had spent the day going to currency traders on Robson Street and buying ourselves another set of dress clothes. The sky had been overcast, threatening rain, but now the sun had dipped below the clouds and there was a relaxed feeling in the air. Our room looked out over English Bay, and there was an otherworldly hue cast by the orange glow of the setting sun. Jay and I had just had sex on the queen-sized bed and were now settled in lounge chairs looking out over the bay.

Jay poured himself a glass of port and carded out a few lines of coke. After we did our lines we moved onto the balcony to enjoy the last of the sunlight. The scene was perfect: two lovers alone in our hotel room, nobody knowing where we were or how to get hold of us. The sun seemed to be setting for us alone, so complete was our universe of two.

As Jay finished his port, I opened my arm in a sweeping arc and announced to no one in particular, "Just look at all that activity, as though someone were guiding it with an invisible hand." It was a line straight out of my economics textbooks, but I felt it applied to much more than financial markets. I had been watching the rush-hour traffic and marvelling at the realization that there were millions of people here in Vancouver and the

Lower Mainland, but everything seemed to flow smoothly, even though we were all following our personal agendas in life.

I had grown to love Vancouver. In this city I experienced my first lattes, drank Perrier, and ate exotic food from countries whose locations were unknown to me. I ate in a different restaurant every night, receiving tutorials on the world according to Jay and his colleagues. I was beginning to feel more like an adult and less the lost child, and I was completely unaware of how these eight months would forever change me.

7

CURTAIN CALL

SPRING WAS IN THE AIR, and our time in Whistler was coming to an end. Jay and I had packed up the condo for the summer and were on our way back to our seasonal jobs in Jasper. We had just spent eight intense months together, but now we weren't getting along. We had no road map for the future. I knew that it was going to be difficult for me to go back to waiting in the wings as Jay returned to his wife and daughter. My life with him felt real, and I no longer wanted to hide our relationship. I brought this up as we sped down Highway 1 toward the Coast Mountains.

"We've been together for almost a year," I said. "If you can't tell her now, I need to know how long you're planning to wait."

Jay, as usual, responded with irritation. "It's not that simple. You think you have all the information, but you don't. You think the world is black and white, but it's not. You need to trust me. I'll know when the timing is right."

But I was tired of waiting, so I pressed him. The exchange became more heated as we drove, and Jay finally blew up, telling me more than I think he'd planned to say.

"You knew the deal when you got involved with me," he blurted as he pulled into a hotel parking lot in Hope. "If I leave Liz, she'll move back east and I'll never see my kid again. And my cover will be blown. Instead of being the stable family man, I'll just have you. And you're a loose cannon on deck."

I didn't know quite how to take this. I didn't want to be like his wife, who stayed at home and complained that her husband was never around. I wanted action, adventure, romance. In this respect, Jay and I were more suited to each other, but he told me time and again that I could never be the anchor for him that his wife and daughter were. Whenever he said this it confused me, because it blatantly contradicted the promise he had been making to me ever since we met: that he would leave Liz to be with me as soon as the time was right.

Now, sitting in the truck, I realized that there was no contradiction at all in Jay's actions. He had no intention of leaving his wife, which meant that he had been stringing me along ever since we met almost a year earlier. I also realized that everything I thought I knew about him could well be a lie.

We parked the truck outside the hotel and walked into the lobby to rent a room for the night. As a result of the cocaine, which we were still using regularly, and the tension in our relationship, we had no desire to eat anything. We lay down on the bed without exchanging any more words, but I couldn't go to sleep. I was lying beside a man I realized I didn't know, and whom I now didn't trust. I tried to remember where he'd put his guns—were they in the room with him?—and for the first time in our relationship I feared for my life. I felt he knew something I did not, and that he was getting all of his ducks in a row for some upcoming change. I was still in love with Jay, but I was beginning to wonder if I had let myself be elaborately used and betrayed. After lying awake for what seemed like hours, I finally fell asleep.

The next morning we drove to a pancake house for waffles and coffee. We alternately stared at each other over our platters and pretended to read the paper. A couple of police officers came into the restaurant and did a double take on seeing Jay. We couldn't tell if it was because they sensed something or thought they recognized him, but we both noticed and got out of there as fast as we could. I felt trapped. I did not want to be leaving with Jay, but I knew I could not go to the cops either.

We jumped into the truck and drove for seven hours until we reached Jasper. The entire time I reminded Jay of his promise that he would leave Liz.

"You're forcing my hand," he repeated whenever I brought the issue up. But I felt the opposite: he was forcing *my* hand by refusing to tell Liz about us. I stared straight ahead and prayed that we would arrive at our destination as quickly as possible. I wanted to get away from this man, who was becoming more of a stranger with each passing moment.

As Jay drove me to our usual drop-off, he said, "I'll be in touch in a few days. Stay calm. We just need to play our cards right and everything will work out fine."

Once again he got to call all the shots. I was growing tired of it. He always had an excuse for keeping things the way they were: we needed things to be just so for the business; we needed such and such to happen so that his family didn't find out about us. When I had time alone in my room to think about the previous eight months, my resentment bubbled to the surface. I was in something deep, I was in it alone, and I did not know how to get out.

Two days later a note arrived in my mailbox: Jay would pick me up at our prescribed meeting place at three o'clock in the afternoon. Unable to resist spending time with him despite my fears, I hopped in his truck. We sped off toward Mount Robson, where there was a piece of land with abandoned cabins on it.

On the drive Jay told me that he needed to bury his surplus cash and some precious metals for safekeeping because "the sands were shifting beneath our feet." He was always talking in abstractions like that. It seemed he could never tell me anything directly, least of all how he felt about us. He pulled rank whenever it suited him, and he forbade me to bring up anything to do with his business when we were inside a vehicle or a building, for fear it had been bugged.

When we arrived at the overgrown entrance to the property, Jay turned the truck onto the lane. After driving about a quarter of a mile we crossed some railroad tracks, and the cabins came into view. As soon as we were parked, Jay stepped out of the truck and grabbed a shovel and a square Tupperware container filled with U.S. dollars and gold. I followed him into the woods. After walking for five minutes, he put the box on the ground and began to dig.

"Why are we doing this?" I asked, finally unable to stifle the question.

"Because we don't know what will happen," Jay replied. "I can't keep this much loot in my house anymore. If anything happens to me, you'll have a way to get to where you need to go, to get your life on another track."

I knew that this was as much detail as I was going to get out of him, so I let the conversation die. I took a turn digging the hole, and when it was deep enough we placed the box in it and shovelled dirt to fill the hole. We returned to the truck, threw the spade in the rear, and headed back to Jasper so Jay could be home in time for dinner.

When he dropped me off, I walked over to Tara's apartment. Sensing that something was wrong, she made a pot of tea and sat down in the arm-chair beside me. I knew the safest thing was to tell no one about what I had been through for the past eight months, but I needed an ally, someone to help me sort through what I saw as a dilemma. So I told her everything.

Her eyes became big and round, but she didn't say a word until I was done. Then all she could muster was "Holy shit. You've got yourself into a mess this time."

"I'm scared," I told her. "And I don't trust him anymore. I'm not sure how far he will take things or what he plans to do next." I told her I was going to write some notes and seal them in an envelope that she should only open if something happened to me. "I need to go back to those cabins to see if the box is still in the ground."

"Right now, at ten o'clock at night? Can't this wait until tomorrow?"

I told her it could only be done in the dark, and that I needed to know now. "If the box is gone, then I'll know for sure that my suspicions are right."

We drove to see a friend who did a lot of construction work and bor-rowed a flashlight and a spade. He kept asking me why I needed them at such an odd hour, and I promised that one day I would tell him, but not that night. Then Tara and I made the forty-five-minute trip out the west highway. We barely spoke; Tara knew I was focused on only one thing. When we arrived, I took out the flashlight and Tara followed me into the woods with the spade. Neither of us voiced our fear, but we were both scared. I found the spot easily, even in the darkness, and began to dig. Tara's eyes were big and round again, and I think that, like me, she felt she was in a movie and not in real life.

I dug down to the bottom of the hole. It was empty. Anger welled up in me at this proof of Jay's deception. I had been questioning certain things about the eight months I had spent with him, but now everything about our affair fell under a shadow of doubt. I filled in the hole, scattering dirt and leaves over the top, and we headed back to the car and to town.

I was freaked—and I was certain that Tara did not comprehend the implications of what we had just found out. Not only did Jay not trust me anymore; he had also involved me in an elaborate scheme to make me believe precisely the opposite. I questioned what his endgame was. He was not a person who did anything without a definite purpose.

After dropping Tara off in front of her apartment, I went back to my room for a long and sleepless night. I spent the next day pondering this new development. By dinnertime I could no longer contain myself. I drove straight to Jay's house, and adrenaline surged through my veins as I walked up to the front door and rang the bell. A young girl—his seven-year-old daughter—opened the door, and I asked her to let her father know he had a visitor. As soon as Jay came to the door and saw me, he grabbed his coat and followed me to the car.

Without saying a word I drove away from his house to a secluded parking lot at the end of town. Then I told Jay what I had done.

He replied, "I knew you were going to do that. That's why I went back and removed the box."

"You're so fucking full of shit!" My voice was subdued, but I could feel anger rumbling to the surface. "You'd better level with me."

He kept telling me to stop forcing his hand, to just let things be and everything would turn out fine.

"You're a fucking lying bastard!" I yelled across the front seat at him. "You've been promising me you'll leave Liz for a year now, and you haven't made one move in that direction yet. You keep telling me that you need her as your cover, so where does that leave me?"

I was going over the edge, and there was nothing Jay hated more than losing control of a situation, especially when that involved emotions.

"You've got a role to play in this too," I insisted. "It's not all just about me being some out-of-control loose cannon on the deck of our *Titanic*."

Jay knew that I had called his bluff and he had to make a decision. "I'm going to go back to the house and tell Liz everything," he said. "Then we'll see where things go from there. Everything will work out fine between us. All you need to do is stay calm and be patient."

I drove him back to his house, then returned to Tara's apartment and stretched out on her couch. I lay awake for hours, going over and over the details of our relationship, trying to figure out whether Jay had ever intended to leave Liz or if he had used that line to suck me in. My mind went around in those circles for hours.

The next day I found a note in my mailbox. Jay wrote that when he told Liz about us, she had threatened to move back east and never let him see his daughter again. She had also threatened to tell the cops everything she knew about his business activities. He ended the note by telling me that we could never see each other again. It was over, and I could never contact him.

My suspicions now turned to certainty: I had been betrayed. I wanted to ask Jay where Liz got the power to keep them together in spite of their agreement to separate if either of them should meet someone else. But I finally realized that it had all been an elaborate lie, that Jay had said and done whatever he needed to say and do to bring me into his world and play me for his own ends. I thought of the months when he had controlled my every move, and unbridled rage rose within me at his duplicity. Through it all he had acted as if he were powerless, when in fact he'd always had a master plan.

I walked back to Tara's apartment for the first in a long string of debriefings. I had nobody else I could talk to about my many unanswered questions, and my already fragile trust in people had all but disintegrated. Luckily Tara was there for me and was completely non-judgmental. We sat and talked, night after night, over pots of tea and simple rice and broccoli dinners. Tara's life was a lot cleaner than mine—drug free, in fact—and it was a welcome respite. For the first time in over a decade, my body got a break from my addictions and overindulgence. As well as being alcohol free, I had stopped using cocaine the day I received Jay's note.

But I still felt drugged, as if my life was not real. I had no idea what to do with my strong and conflicted feelings for Jay. I still loved him, though that love was now tainted with a deep sense of betrayal. At the same time, I was keenly aware that I would soon need to go back to work, despite the fact that I was not sleeping or eating well. Weeks of this deprivation were taking a toll. Whenever I went out to the post office or to do my banking, women would stop me and tell me how great I looked, how thin I was. I wanted to tell them that my secret was an eight-month diet of cocaine followed by betrayal and intense emotional upheaval.

In the end, I went back to work for the trail crew, even though I was thoroughly spent both physically and emotionally and didn't feel strong enough to be wielding a chainsaw all day. I had Tara to talk to, but I still felt completely alone. Jay and the business that he got me involved with had been my world, and that world was gone. I was also crashing from cocaine withdrawal, feeling anxious and irritable, and falling into a delayed depression that is a normal result of altering one's brain chemistry with the drug. I kept going through the motions of my life, but I was losing my grip on any stable or predictable reality and falling into a psychological abyss that deepened with each month.

I had saved enough money to buy a truck that summer, so when my third season with Parks Canada came to an end in the fall of 1989, I packed up my belongings and drove to the West Coast—out to Hornby Island. I needed to see my sister Jane.

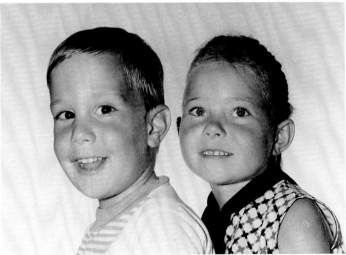

TOP: This is the earliest photo of me. Mom and Dad are seated with (from left to right) me, age one; Karla, age four; and Jane, age two and a half.

BOTTOM: Frankie and I pose for a photo in about 1969.

TOP LEFT: With my siblings in the kitchen of our home in Riverview (left to right): Frankie, Margo, Jane, Karla.

TOP RIGHT: My mom and her first four kids in about 1970. I am standing at the left, with Karla beside me and Jane at right. Frankie is on Mom's lap.

BOTTOM LEFT: My school picture from Grade 4, when I would have been nine or ten.

BOTTOM RIGHT: Me with Richard, the joy of my life, when he was about fifteen months old.

TOP LEFT: My school picture from Grade 8, the year after I started running wild and the year before we moved to Saint John.

TOP RIGHT: Me at fifteen, "the farmer's daughter." This was the year I began keeping a journal as an outlet for my thoughts and emotions.

BOTTOM: In the summer of 1984 I made my way out to the Rockies. Here I am in Jasper's Astoria Hotel Bar. —PHOTO BY SU YOUNG-LESLIE

TOP: My boyfriend Lyle played hockey with his friends on a team called the Bongs. Their girlfriends started their own team, the Bongettes. Here I'm serving up beer to my fellow Bongettes after a hockey game in 1986.

BOTTOM: For Halloween 1987 I dressed up as a mushroom (at right). My friend Charlie was a television set. —PHOTO BY DARCY SHEPPARD

TOP: Standing on the bridge that my crew and I built over Verdant Creek, near Mount Edith Cavell, in the summer of 1988.

BOTTOM: Karen and I returned to Murchison Falls in 1997, the season following my breakdown on the climb, and this time we made a successful ascent. Karen took this picture of me in celebration.

TOP: This shot of me on the lower Weeping Wall was taken the day we filmed Warren's ice climb in March 2003.

BOTTOM: Celebrating the 2003 Canmore Ice Climbing Festival: I'm standing at left with (left to right) Kim Csizmazia, Su Young-Leslie, and Karen McNeill.

TOP: Karen McNeill and Sue Nott after climbing the Cassin Ridge on Denali, in Alaska, 2005. —PHOTO BY JOHN VARCO

BOTTOM: Curtain Call, the grade 6 climb near Jasper with a fracture across the sheet of ice that comprises the last pitch. —PHOTO BY SEAN ELLIOTT

TOP: At the South Pole in January 2005, my first season guiding for Antarctic Logistics and Expeditions.

BOTTOM: Somewhere on the Antarctic Peninsula in March 2005, during my first cruise with Peregrine.

Climbing in Ouray, Colorado, in 2007. —ALAIN DENIS PHOTOGRAPHY

TOP: With my fellow Chicks with Picks guides in 2007 (left to right): Kim Reynolds, Margo Talbot, Kitty Calhoun, Caroline George. —CHRIS GILES PHOTOGRAPHY

BOTTOM: With Warren on a cruise ship en route to South Georgia Island, November 2007.

Karen hamming it up at the base of Cho Oyu, on the Nepal/Tibet border, in 1995.
—PHOTO BY MARG SAUL

8

ACID HOWL

Hornby is one of the many Gulf Islands between the mainland of British Columbia and Vancouver Island. It is approximately nine square miles, and it takes three ferries to get there. Jane was living there with her partner Stepan, and they had a tiny cabin in back of the house. I figured it was the best place to lie low and get my life back on track.

Hornby is populated with what I can only refer to as hippies. In this regard I stood out, and when I arrived, the rumour was that I was a narc. This was the height of irony, but I could see how I must have appeared to the locals: I drove a brand-new vehicle while they were all driving beaters. I dressed in jeans and jean jackets, white-collared shirts and cowboy boots; they dressed in Guatemalan clothing and Peruvian woollens. And I appeared to have more disposable income than just about anyone else my age. But I didn't care about fitting in or making friends. I had moved to Hornby to hide out, lie low, and figure out where to go from here. My life had been moving so fast that I could hardly keep up, let alone take stock of where I had come from, what I was doing and where I was headed.

It had been almost two years since I had taken my last drink. When I first quit, I'd had dreams every night in which I was tempted with alcohol—people were offering me drinks or handing me cups of coffee laced with alcohol. These dreams went on for the first six months, and variations on the theme continued for the next year and a half. But shortly after I moved to Hornby I began having different dreams. I heard a voice telling me that I was as controlled by alcohol in my complete avoidance of it as I had been when I could not go a day without it. At first I ignored these dreams and decided they were just another form of my earlier temptation dreams. But they persisted, and I became curious to know if their message might in fact be true. I discussed it with Jane, and she agreed that it made sense, however strange it sounded. So on March 27, 1990, Jane and I split a beer in the company of her friends in celebration of my twenty-sixth birthday.

I had once told a psychologist that the first time I drank alcohol was the first time I'd experienced feelings other than pain and anger. It was as though these positive emotions were frozen inside, and the alcohol was allowing them to move again. He said this was the most common observation he heard from alcoholics. But on the night I shared a beer with Jane, as I took my first sip since quitting, I did not experience the overwhelming onslaught of feelings that I had in the past. I believe the reason I could now take a drink without risk is that I had learned how to feel the full gamut of emotions during my time of sobriety with Jay—first with my feelings of love for him and then with the pain of our separation. I had addressed the issue that had driven me to drink in the first place: alcohol had once been the anaesthetic that dulled the painful feelings I stuffed down inside me, as well as a lubricant for the more positive feelings that I had no idea how to access on my own.

I hadn't talked to my parents for over a year, so I called soon after my birthday. I wanted to appear normal; I didn't want people finding out that I never spoke to my parents, as this would clearly suggest there was something wrong. At the same time I was reluctant to call them: neither of them would talk about anything of relevance to me, especially my childhood, which is where I was beginning to suspect the root of my psychological problems lay. My mother still believed I'd gone crazy at puberty, although she would not discuss this with me either. The only other information I had was my memories, and hearing my siblings and peers repeatedly tell me that I was "off the rails" and a "loose cannon" made me wonder if in fact the problem lay inside me.

My mother picked up the phone and we talked for over an hour—or, rather, she talked at me. She wasn't interested in anything to do with me or my life but rambled on endlessly about Frankie. When she spoke about any-thing happening in the outside world, it was in a negative way, as if there was nothing good in the world. I had that familiar sinking feeling when I put the phone down, and within hours I was in the bathroom throwing up. I assumed it was my ulcer again, but Jane insisted that it wasn't a coincidence and that I really should look into the connection. I promised her I would.

There were a lot of New Age healers on Hornby, so I decided to consult one. For months I had been driving by a house with a sign on the front door, *Aura Reader*. I'd made jokes about it every time I saw it. Although I didn't really know what an aura reader did, I decided it couldn't be any less fruitful than my experiences with psychologists and psychiatrists. On the day of my appointment, I closed my eyes while the aura reader did an assessment of my energy field. As soon as she spoke I knew that she had seen something significant. "Your aura is red. All I see is anger. It's block-ing everything else out that you could be experiencing in your life." She mentioned a few more things, but anger was the main issue. When I left her place I felt that I had a good idea what the problem was. However, I had no idea what to do about it.

I continued to spend a lot of time alone. Not only did I read every book I could find by Noam Chomsky, but I also read books by other criti-cal thinkers, especially Wilhelm Reich, the one-time protegé of Sigmund Freud, who focused on character structure rather than on individual neu-rotic symptoms as the root of mental imbalance. Just about every day I went to the ocean for long walks. My focus slowly shifted away from Jay. As I started to meet people, I realized I was living on an island populated mostly by artists and farmers who were interested in philosophy, politics, and social causes. When spring came, I began working with a local farmer and tasted organic food for the first time. It was a healing time for me; I wasn't drinking much alcohol, but neither was I avoiding it. I was doing a bit of coke whenever it surfaced, but not in amounts that worried me.

Then I started dating a man named Al, who was a partier, and this ratcheted up my intake of intoxicating substances. By the time my second winter on Hornby rolled around, I found myself in that familiar pattern of coping with an emotionally remote lover, which caused my fear of aban-donment to surface, along with my feelings that I was not worthy or loved.

I was still choosing men who were emotionally unavailable, as well as men who were much older than me: Lyle by twelve years, Jay by ten, and Al by fourteen. Perhaps I was trying to find the father figure that I had never had, but the replacements were as unavailable as the one I had grown up with.

I felt the urge to run away, and since there were no mountains nearby, I packed everything into my truck and ran all the way back to Alberta. Returning to Jasper, I felt at home, just as I had the first time I arrived, years before. I loved the cool air, the stunning views, and all the physical activities available in the mountains. For the next five months I went back and forth between Hornby and Jasper, unable to decide where to live or what to do.

During one of my stays in Jasper I met Carl, who had just come back from San Francisco with sheets of blotter acid. Although I hadn't done any acid since my university days, I had always been attracted to the highs it produced. I felt it opened up interesting states of consciousness that I had always wanted to revisit, but I didn't trust the quality of the drug on the street. Carl assured me his acid was of the finest quality—he had gotten the sheets from a friend who ran a lab in San Francisco—and he said it was best to get away from civilization for the high.

We decided to do a hit on a cross-country ski trip up Portal Creek and toward the Tonquin Valley. After packing our knapsacks with a snack and some water, we drove the forty-five minutes south of town to the trailhead. We were just beginning to feel the effects of the acid as we waxed our skis and got onto the trail. On those early trips the acid would come on pretty quickly, but slowly enough for me to notice that the world I knew was fading away to be replaced by an exceptionally vibrant and magical one. I was relieved to feel that sense of happiness I had felt the first time I took acid with Kate, seven years earlier in Halifax. I was reminded of the definition of ecstasy—"to stand outside oneself"—and felt that the key to freeing myself from a constant state of anxiety was to work through my emotions with the goal of eliminating their oppressive effect on me.

Carl and I skied uphill and into the valley for hours, without eating or drinking. That was another miraculous thing about acid: my body seemed to be using a different type of energy while I was under its effect. Not only did we not eat or drink, I didn't even have the urge to urinate. The overriding feeling was of freedom: from bodily demands and the culture's "group mind," but most importantly from my emotional turmoil.

We turned around and started our ski out. Although it had felt like a gentle grade on the way in, we quickly picked up speed as we careened around corners and negotiated the straightaways. My body felt light, empty, unburdened, and so too did my mind. I experienced it as living in pure joy, where there was no yesterday or tomorrow, and where the present moment was so captivating that there was no desire for anything else. When we returned to the truck, our cheeks were ablaze from the cool wind and our eyes sparkled with excitement. It had been six hours since we had taken the hit, and Carl assured me that the intensity of the high would now begin to mellow. We drove into town and went straight to the Astoria Bar, a place where I had spent a lot of time since arriving in Jasper so many years earlier.

We walked into the bar and sat at one of the round tables toward the back. When the waitress came by, we ordered two glasses of red wine. Carl had explained to me that a drink would take the edge off as we came down from our trip. I was impressed with how rationally he approached the drug, something I had never done in the past. He figured out all the details so we could maximize our time on the drug and minimize the effects of coming down.

For the next three months, Carl and I did acid during the day and came down over a bottle of wine in the evening. We did this an average of four days a week, and as the weeks went by we found ourselves increasing the number of hits we would take in any one session. Sometimes we took the drug later in the day and stayed up all night. We skied into backcountry cabins in the Fryatt and Tonquin valleys and stayed for several days, skiing and doing acid. When Carl was preparing to go up north to work for the summer, he left me some acid so I could continue my journey.

Not long afterward, a funny thing began to happen: I started breaking down, crying uncontrollably, anywhere, anytime—in the backcountry, in cafés, in bars. A floodgate had burst and I could no longer contain my emotion. I cut back on my acid intake, thinking that perhaps these breakdowns and my frequent use of acid could be related. I remembered stories from the sixties about people losing their minds by using too many drugs, and I got worried. Although there was no passion between Carl and me, I found him to be as cold and remote as my lovers. He reminded me of my mother. All these things were a maelstrom swirling around my head. If I'd had a stable place to live I might have coped better, but I was either living in my truck or staying at Carl's friends' place. After Carl left town, my breakdowns continued. Alone and afraid of what was happening to me, I checked myself into the hospital.

I was immediately given my own bed in the outpatient's unit and cried uncontrollably from the minute I was checked in. When the nurses came into my room to check on me, I felt grateful for their care. They asked me if I knew what was happening, to which I truthfully answered no. They reassured me, told me to do whatever I had to do and that everything would be fine—not to worry. After hours of being wracked by a grief deeper than I'd ever known, I felt empty and quiet. Eventually I drifted off to sleep.

The following morning a doctor came in to see me. Sitting on the edge of my bed, she began to talk with me. Did I know what had precipitated checking myself into the hospital? I replied that the only connection popping up for me was the fact that I had just spent three months with a man who reminded me of my mother, and this had triggered a tsunami of pain from my childhood. I wasn't about to mention that I had done dozens of hits of acid in a matter of months.

"I feel fine now," I told her. "I'll check out as soon as we're done talking."

She suggested that I make an appointment with a psychologist instead, so I let her make one for me.

The meeting with the psychologist came and went, but my depression stayed. I was beginning to realize that knowing what the problem was intellectually, and talking about it with professionals, could only take me so far. I needed to make a shift at a profound level, but I had no idea how to do this. I began reading spiritual texts, and intuited that because the problem had its roots in the psyche, it could only be resolved by probing more deeply. Meanwhile, I continued breaking down, crying uncontrollably anywhere and anytime, and it began happening more often.

Whenever I felt an episode coming on, I would get in my truck and drive to a secluded spot outside town, go into the woods, and scream at the trees, the rocks, the sky. It felt like the safest place to express my turbulent emotions. I decided that I could not afford to keep doing acid, and I admitted to myself that my fragile state was undoubtedly related to my doing so much of the drug.

Two months after my hospital visit, my moods began to stabilize. I spent most of my time alone, parked at pullout areas away from town. I had everything I needed with me: my backcountry stove and pots, dried foodstuffs, a warm bed, and all of my warm clothing. I went into town only to replenish my food or to spend some time reading at the local café.

Around this time I noticed a pattern in my depression. One feeling always accompanied the black wave that descended on me whenever I was about to fall into the abyss: powerlessness. I also noticed that anger accompanied my resurfacing from these black states. I began to view my anger in a new way, as an ally that I could use to propel myself away from that which was no longer serving me—whether it was a state of mind, a situation, or another person—and back into the centre of my personal power.

When I resurfaced from this latest round of depression and breakdowns, I felt euphoric, elated, and very social. After living in a state of profound isolation for months, I swung into the opposite mood, a desire to have close, intimate contact with life, which would prove to be as dangerous as the other. In this period of mania I cast caution aside. My risky behaviour might take the form of using a new substance or sleeping with a virtual stranger. This would send the pendulum of my moods on a skyrocketing swing and set me up for another crash. I was living my life on the edge, where I attained balance only rarely and briefly.

During this phase I went to the bar with some friends and met Doug, a carpenter, who had recently moved back to Jasper after spending two years in Valemount, a small town nearby in British Columbia. Doug was really cute, about my height, and well built. He was fun, and funny. We had been in the bar for a few hours when he leaned over and told me he was still renting the place in Valemount. We could drive out there and spend the night, if I wanted to. I didn't reply right away, but I already knew I would leave with him. When everyone else had left the bar, we walked to my truck and began the long drive out the west highway.

For reasons that will always be a mystery to me, Doug broke through every sexual inhibition I had ever had. He was a hedonist, and he moved slowly and deliberately through every tiny ritual of the sexual act. We spent four days in bed, and nothing existed in the world except the intertwining of our bodies. After that we spent our weekends in Valemount, having sex and doing drugs. I had rekindled my appetite for other substances when I decided to stop doing acid, and by the time I met Doug I was imbibing a potpourri of drugs, including cocaine. When Doug discovered this, he taught me another way to ingest coke, a method called "freebasing."

Initially I worked with Doug, and we did a string of small carpentry jobs through the spring. Then I heard about a woman who ran a landscaping company in town and got a job with her. Suzie was slightly shorter than me, with straight brown hair and brown eyes. She was one of the few women I have met who was more muscular than me. She had broad cheekbones and laughed more than any other woman too. The word I always thought of when I was around her was "earthy." She exuded an innocent sensuality and had a killer sense of humour, so what started off as a work relationship soon became a solid friendship.

The biggest strain on our friendship was the frequency with which I did not show up for work. At first the issue was my infatuation with Doug and our little hideaway west of town. But as the summer moved along I was getting more heavily into drugs again, as well as selling some pot to help pay for my addictions. I had also begun drinking more than I had intended when I went off the wagon the previous year.

About three months into my relationship with Doug, we were spending the weekend in Valemount, as usual. It was noon, and he had already started cooking up freebase in the kitchen, using a combination of cocaine, baking soda, and water. Having been up all night doing the drug, I believed it was too early to start smoking it again, so I decided to go out into the backyard and tan. I was not feeling as good as I thought I should feel, and I knew it was because of my overindulgence in drugs and alcohol. I was doing acid, mushrooms, cocaine, and freebase on a regular basis, as well as drinking every day. I was accustomed to a huge intake of substances, but it was taking its toll. I felt numb and flat. Some sort of life spark had disappeared, and I thought maybe I could retrieve some of it by spending time in the sun.

The yard was completely fenced in, so I took off my white cotton shirt, rolled down the top of my one-piece bathing suit, and lay back in the plastic lounge chair. I heard children laughing, and I knew they were in the yard next door, but I thought nothing further of it until I heard a car pull up in our driveway.

I was instantly on the alert. Not only did nobody know where we were, but we had a lot of drugs in the house. I pulled up the top of my suit, put on my shirt, and walked through the gate just in time to see a cop at the back door talking with Doug.

I was freaked, but I kept my composure as Doug calmly spoke to the cop as though I was not there. The cop explained that he had received a call from the neighbour, complaining that her kids were watching me sunbathe in the nude through the slits in the fence. He said that Doug should let me know it was illegal to be nude where anyone from the public could see you, including in your own backyard.

"Can't you control her?" I heard him ask Doug. "She should go live in the bush if she wants to act like that." He shot me a look as he returned to his car.

I went inside to ask Doug about their conversation, but I was seething. "What the fuck!" I yelled at him when I was certain that the cop had driven off. "What the fuck are you thinking, cooking up this early in the day. What if he had decided to come into the house, or knew what burning freebase smelled like?"

Doug reminded me that it had been my actions, not his, that had brought the police to the house in the first place. I left the house and went out for a walk. I was angry, not only at Doug, but also at the highly addictive drug he had introduced me to, at the cops, and at the world. I felt that things were closing in on me, and this close call had woken up something inside me. Finally I calmed down, went back to the house, and opened a beer. When Doug handed me the homemade coke-can pipe, I took it.

That evening we were drinking and smoking freebase at the house when I told Doug that I wanted to drive to Jasper that night instead of the next morning. Since I would be doing the driving, he agreed, although he would rather have stayed and smoked some more. He fell asleep shortly after we pulled out of Valemount.

About halfway to Jasper there is a body of water called Moose Lake. It is on the south side of the highway, near Mount Robson. The moon was full, and I could see the ten-thousand-foot relief of the mountain's south face, with its snow- and ice-capped summit shining in the moonlight. The scene took my breath away. I looked over at the lake, with the moon hovering above and the reflection in the water, and I was overcome by the beauty of it all.

The freebase was wearing off, and I wanted to pull over and smoke some more. Instead I did something I had never done in my life: I prayed to God. If you had asked me, I would have told you I did not believe in God, but I was desperate. Besides, there were millions of people in the world who claimed that prayer worked. I remembered my experience at fourteen, when I had heard the stars promise to watch over me. That had made a strong impact on me, and I wondered if I in turn could speak to the stars. So while I was driving, I looked at the stars and spoke to them silently. I told whatever power was out there that if it took this feeling of craving away, I would never touch freebase again. To my amazement, the feeling disappeared immediately, and I spent the rest of the drive knowing that no matter what else happened, I was not going to touch a substance that addictive ever again. I also knew that this experience, like my experience with the stars at fourteen, had shown me there existed in the universe a power that was greater than anything I had previously known. All I had to do now was figure out how to tap into it.

In the meantime, I soon realized that in order to keep this promise, I had to leave Doug. As I was moving away from drugs, he was getting more heavily into them. I had also had a dream in which I had gotten busted for selling pot, and I started to worry that it might actually come true. I didn't know what my next move was, but I knew it was time for a different strategy.

9

SHADES OF BEAUTY

I WAS TWO MONTHS SHY of my twenty-eighth birthday and still living in my truck and dealing drugs. I had kept the promise I'd made to myself never to freebase cocaine again, but I had no problem continuing to do my other drugs of choice. And I was drinking because the best place for me to sell drugs was at the bar, where everyone could get hold of me. That's where I connected with Paul. I had known him for years, but he had an air of unapproachability that had kept me at bay. Little by little, though, we interacted through mutual acquaintances until we had formed enough of a relationship to discover a shared attraction.

As far as my sexual initiation was concerned, Paul took over where Doug had left off. It was the most intense and passionate sex I had ever had, but our passion was a double-edged sword. Paul's rage and mine were a volatile combination. We were two deeply traumatized people coming together without any idea of the destruction we were capable of causing. We triggered each other's rage and pain continuously and mixed it up with too much alcohol and too many drugs. What initially seemed to be a match made in heaven was only the mirror image of my internally devastated self.

People stayed away from us, mostly because they took the anger in our eyes to mean that we wanted to beat them up. Sometimes we did. For the two years we were together we got into many fights, with outsiders and between ourselves. We were also a magnet for cops. On my own I wasn't much of a threat, but I can only imagine the effect Paul and I together had on those around us.

We were under surveillance in bars as we both had a history of causing disturbances. The cops would approach me easily enough, but they were intimidated by Paul, who was six feet tall and two hundred pounds of solid muscle, with blue eyes that radiated an inner wildness. He had a reputation in that town: on one occasion he had fought off four bouncers at the Athabasca Hotel, all at once. Another time he was taken to the local police station after being subdued with pepper spray because he had been demolishing an abandoned house with his bare hands and a wooden club. When the police finally got him into their car, he proceeded to tear up the interior of the vehicle.

Jasper had a reputation as well. A town of about four thousand people, it boasts one of North America's highest per capita rates of alcohol and drug consumption, as well as a high incidence of suicide. Since it is a tourist destination, news of these unique claims doesn't make it beyond the town limits, because those facts would spoil the beautiful Rocky Mountain resort image that the town relies on for a large portion of its revenue. Other than the families that live there full time, Jasper's residents are largely young people who come to work in the tourist industry. And among these people there are a handful of climbers.

By the time I met him, Paul had been climbing for ten years. His passion was for ice climbing, an obscure sport in which ice axes and crampons are used to scale frozen waterfalls. I had known of the sport's existence for a few years before I met Paul, and I had always been intrigued by it but had never tried it. Two weeks after we got together, we drove forty-five minutes south on the Icefields Parkway to my first ice climb. It was almost noon when we started the hike in to a strip of ice known as Melt Out.

I followed Paul along the trail in my new Scarpa double-plastic boots. We had spent the previous week finding all the gear I would need for my introduction to the sport. Now I was excited to feel the snow under my feet squeak in the cold February morning. Although the trail took us uphill, it was not steep. Before twenty minutes had passed I caught my first glimpse of waterfall ice, a beautiful sight. I had imagined it would look whitish grey, like ice cubes in a freezer, but this strip was wide and blue and shone like a gem in the midday sun.

We stopped at the base of the ice and took off our packs. I followed each of Paul's actions as he got ready for the climb. I put on my down jacket first, so I would not cool off too much, and then my helmet, followed by my harness. Paul told me to tighten the laces on my boots before putting on my crampons. He explained that while we wanted our boots to be loose when walking, we needed them to be snug for climbing, or our heels would drop and our footwork would become sloppy. Lastly, we put on our crampons.

Paul picked up the rope that he had laid in the snow and began uncoiling it off to the side. He explained how to flake out the rope so that it would move freely without getting tangled while the leader was climbing. Then he showed me how to tie into the rope with a figure-eight knot. When he had finished his knot, he helped me tie myself into the other end. Then he showed me how to put the rope into my figure-eight device, how to feed the rope through for the leader, and how the braking action worked to catch a fall should one occur.

I was mesmerized by the whole affair: the gear, the ice, and the cold air that made me feel alive. I felt at peace standing at the base of that ice strip, on the side of a mountain, surrounded by the beauty of nature. My recent experience communicating with the stars still resonated, as did a deep belief that there was a power in the universe greater than us. For me, spending time in the wilderness had become synonymous with tapping into this power. Here, standing at the base of my first waterfall ice climb, Paul introduced me to a whole new way of relating to the mountains and nature.

Paul had warned me that climbing was inherently dangerous and that I had to be as aware as possible during the activity. He told me never to let my guard down, because that was when mistakes were made, and mistakes could be very costly to a climber dangling from a rope high above the ground.

Satisfied that I would do a good job of it, Paul set off up the ice. I watched and listened as he started climbing. First he swung his axes into the ice, and then he stepped up by setting his crampons into the ice. He removed one of his axes, placed it above his head, leaned out, and stepped his feet up. Taking out his other axe, he repeated the same movements until he had reached the top of the climb. I watched as he put in an anchor consisting of two ice screws, clipped himself in, and told me that he was off belay. I took my belay device off the rope and walked over to where my axes were lying on the ground. Paul began pulling up the slack in the rope while I got ready to climb by strapping my gloved hands into the leashes of my tools. Moments after the rope came taut, I heard Paul telling me that I was on belay.

I swung into the ice. It came naturally to me because I had done carpentry work and was familiar with how to swing a hammer. I loved the inherent aggression of piercing my tool into the ice, and I proceeded to swing the other one in as well. Looking down at my feet, I brought them up onto the sheet of ice and then took one of my axes out and placed it above my head, just as Paul had done. I was immediately captivated by the rhythmic pleasure of the activity, the sound of metal hitting ice, and the complete absorption of my mind and my senses. I loved the smoothness of the ice and the performance of my equipment. Partway up the pitch, I realized that this was the perfect outlet for the intensity that I constantly lived with but had no idea what to do with.

Before I knew it, I was at the anchor and Paul was showing me how to clip into it and get everything ready for the rappel. He said he was going to be lowering me on this climb, but the next day we would go to another more involved climb and he would teach me how to rappel, as well as the other skills I needed to be a safe climbing partner. When I got back down to the ground, Paul told me to step to the side so I wouldn't be hit by any falling ice as he rappelled.

As I moved over to where we had left our packs, I noticed that I felt large inside, expanded, as though my world had just become bigger than it had ever been. I also felt solid; I had just accomplished something using my own strength, and this gave me a feeling of confidence. I was having fun, and for once I hadn't had to ingest huge quantities of illicit substances to achieve that state.

Soon Paul was on the ground beside me. We both smiled as we took off our gear and put it back into our packs for the hike down to the highway and the drive back to town.

The following morning dawned clear and cold, and once again we drove the forty-five minutes south to a three-tiered climb called Shades of Beauty. This time I could see the climb as we pulled to the side of the road. It looked much farther away, and a lot higher, than our previous day's climb. When we got out of the truck, Paul explained that each tier or curtain was a pitch of climbing. There were ledges between each of the steps where he would stop and put in a belay. Although it would be a longer and harder climb than the one the day before, he felt that I would be fine, considering my seemingly natural ability on ice.

Once again we grabbed our packs and started the hike in. The approach was flat at first, and I found myself focusing on the sound of my footsteps and the feel of the cold air on my face. I felt alive and excited about my new-found activity. This was the closest I had ever come to being happy without using drugs. I felt a sense of freedom when I climbed, and I didn't miss the fact that, unlike many of my previous activities, this one was *good* for me. I was getting large doses of fresh air and sunshine, and my muscles were being used much more than they ever had. I had a glow from the sun, wind, and cold, and this flush made me look healthier than I probably was.

Soon we were at the base of the waterfall. I could see that this climb was substantially steeper than the one the day before, but Paul told me not to worry—I was plenty strong and could follow him up the climb. We geared up quickly now that I didn't need to be told what to do, and within fifteen minutes we were once again ready to climb. I watched Paul go up the first section, and though it was much the same as the day before, I took note of all the little tricks. I noticed that Paul took his axe out whenever he did not like his placement. He would use the same hole but swing into it to get more of the pick inserted. I also saw how he chose places to put his feet: he put them on features like little ledges, not just anywhere on the blank steep sections of ice.

When I commented on this, he told me to do the same, to try to use his old placements both for my axes and my crampons. "You'll save a ton of energy that way. There's no need to make new placements when mine are right in front of your eyes."

Paul was in a much better mood when he was climbing. He was often prone to periods of dark brooding and angry outbursts, but out on the ice he was more centred and grounded.

When it was my turn to climb I wasted no time moving over to where Paul had set out and swung my axes into the ice. That feeling of freedom swept over me again, and I knew that this was going to be my new focus in life. Though Paul was the more experienced climber and the one who put the rope up for me, when I began climbing it was entirely up to me to use my physical and mental power to get to the top of each pitch.

I found climbing so engaging that everything else slipped away, including the weight of the world that often felt heavy on my shoulders. I recognized in these first two climbs an outlet for my anger. Long ago I had learned that although expressing anger was permissible for men in our culture, it was taboo for women. But here was an activity in which my innate aggression was actually beneficial.

The main attraction, by far, was that I got to spend inordinate amounts of time in the mountains, pursuing an activity that was so demanding it kept my energy moving and the dark clouds at bay. By the end of the second day, all I wanted to do was climb as much ice as I possibly could before it melted away.

10

DANCING WITH CHAOS

MY DESIRE TO CLIMB ICE CONSTANTLY was fulfilled as Paul and I climbed ice by day and camped in the day-use shelters by night. These shelters had been built all along the highways of the Rocky Mountain national parks and were well stocked with firewood. We lived in my truck for the rest of the winter, hanging plastic tarps over the shelter doors, lighting the giant wood stove inside, and cooking meals and drying out our gear. When night descended we pulled the foam mattress out of the truck and slept in comfort on the floor of the shelter. We had a two-person bivi sack that we would get into in our sleeping bags, staying warm when the temperatures outside were in the minus double digits. We spent all week climbing ice and returned to town on weekends to replenish our stocks and imbibe our favourite substances. But during one of these trips back to town, I made an error in judgment that quickly sent me into another downward spiral.

Paul and I were in the Astoria Bar on February 14, 1992. I remember the date, not because Valentine's Day holds any special significance for me, but because AIDS Jasper was handing out free condoms that night. It was Happy Hour, and we had just returned from a two-week trip in the mountains. I hadn't seen anyone but Paul for fourteen days and was eager to drink and socialize.

I was standing beside the back bar holding a gin and tonic, listening to music and chatting with friends. When my drink ran out, I decided to cross the floor to the main bar because it had a shorter lineup. I was stopped along the way by a tall, well-built man who started up a conversation. He told me his name was Kevin and he was a construction worker from Edmonton. This was his first time in Jasper, and he asked me a few questions about the best places to eat, the coolest hangouts for the locals, et cetera. And then he mentioned having trouble finding drugs in town and asked me if I knew where to get some. I laughed at the idea that it was hard to find drugs in Jasper and asked him what he wanted.

"I'd really like to find some coke," he replied.

It had been only a few months since I'd left Doug, but in that time I had divested myself of cocaine and swore I would never touch it again. "I have no idea where you can get cocaine; I think it's the evilest drug on the planet," I said, but Kevin told me he would be happy to find anything for the weekend. I said I would go over to the bar at the Athabasca Hotel and find him a quarter ounce of pot.

Ever since I had dreamed about getting busted, I had focused on ridding myself of my remaining stash. Valentine's Day evening found me with just one quarter-ounce bag of marijuana left to sell. So when a construction worker from Edmonton, whom I had never seen before and never expected to see again, asked if I knew where he could find some pot, I broke the first rule in the drug-dealing world: I sold to someone I didn't know. I left the bar, went to my truck, and retrieved that last baggie of pot. Within minutes I was completing the transaction, and I was now drug free. As soon as Kevin handed me the money, I walked to the back of the bar, ordered a double gin and tonic, and resumed drinking and socializing with my friends. I had no idea what I had just done, and wouldn't know for another month.

Kevin immediately went to the police station to file a report. He was actually an undercover narcotics officer, brought in because the local cops were having trouble busting any of Jasper's drug dealers. The officers handed the case to a junior constable straight out of training in Saskatchewan. They told him only to watch me—it wasn't worth busting me if I had gotten the pot from someone else. But the constable in charge of my case was green, and he thought he had a case that would be a great start to his career. He waited only three weeks before putting out a warrant for my arrest. Because he did not know my last name, and because I didn't have a fixed address, he had trouble finding me. But on the morning of March 14, as Paul and I were coming out of Mountain Foods Café, I ran into Doug.

"The cops are looking for you," he told me. "They say it's something about your sister out on the coast."

I hadn't spoken to any of my family for a while, and I panicked at the thought that something had happened to Jane. Paul walked with me as far as the soccer field across from the police station, and I told him I'd see him back there soon.

Then I strolled into the police station and told them who I was and why I had come. Several officers were standing around and looking at me. The chief of police for the detachment was summoned. He asked me if I knew why I was there, and I said I'd heard that they wanted to talk to me about my sister. He replied that I was under arrest for trafficking in a narcotic. My mind raced, trying to think of how this had happened, how they had found out. The chief then told me the story, and the night in the bar came flashing back to me.

"I probably don't need to read you your rights," he said. "You've probably seen enough TV shows by now to know what they are."

In fact I didn't know what my rights were. I was way too nervous to remember details from movies; I couldn't believe what was happening to me. The chief told me that I would be strip-searched and fingerprinted before they put me in a holding cell. He took the water bottle I had brought with me out of my hands and reached out to take my jacket from me. He then motioned to the cops standing around the room.

When I realized what was happening, I got dead calm. What else could I do when I was being plucked out of my ordinary everyday life and thrown into jail? I was ushered into a small room made of steel, with one small window in the door. A female cop strip-searched me as the male cops talked and laughed outside the door. There was an electricity in the air, and I got the distinct feeling the cops were enjoying busting me.

The strip search was the most degrading experience I have ever had. I took off all my clothing and laid it on the steel table. The woman who was searching me whispered that she was sorry she had to do this and she could see no reason for it, as I was clearly not any threat to them. She was the only evidence of humanity I'd noticed since walking into the police station.

When she was finished, I got dressed, and she brought me back into the main room of the detachment. She handed me off to the young constable, who took my fingerprints before escorting me to my cell. It was the size of a large bathroom. The walls were concrete. There was a little cot with no blankets, an open toilet, and a sink. The bars were black iron and half the thickness of my wrist, and as the constable closed the door there was a heavy sound to the latch.

I stood in my cell in disbelief, wondering what I was supposed to do now. Paul was sitting in the park waiting for me. When I did not come out, he would know what had happened. I was so freaked that I remained calm; there was nothing to do but lie down on the cold mattress and review the situation. What I thought about was how I missed the fresh air and the warmth of sunlight on my face. Now all I had was a man-made tomb that was closing in around me. I knew I could live without most things that human beings deemed necessary in their lives, but I could never thrive without my connection to nature. Nature was my sustainer, my healer, perhaps the only thing worth staying free (and alive) for. I swore that I would relish the feel of wind on my face and cold in my bones for the rest of my life. But for now I had only one goal: regaining my freedom. I prayed, for the second time in my life, in the desperate hope that I would get out of this jail cell before the night was through.

I heard footsteps and looked up to see the constable in charge of my case on the other side of the cell door. Throwing his ring of keys into the air and catching them again, over and over, he said they had so much information on me that they could easily keep me locked up for ten years. He told me the only way I could avoid this was by providing information on who I had gotten the drugs from. I remained calm, but I nervously wondered just how much they knew.

I asked to make a phone call but was told I had to wait until they had finished with all the paperwork. Eventually the chief came to my cell, unlocked the door, and took me into a room with a desk and a telephone. I dialled a friend who would know what to do. I told him I was in jail and that my only hope of getting out was his gathering enough money for my bail. He replied that he would see what he could do, and I knew he would do everything in his power to get me out of there quickly; we both knew that the longer I sat in a jail cell, the more I would be tempted to give in to pressure and bargain for my release.

Now I just had to wait for the police to get hold of a justice of the peace, who would determine if I was to be released and, if so, under what parameters. I was relieved when a JP arrived around 10 p.m. to rule on my behalf. I learned that, under most circumstances, no JP would have driven the fifty miles to Jasper at that late hour to get a drug dealer out of jail. The fact that I was a woman played in my favour: the justice couldn't abide the thought of a lone girl lying in jail all night. She wanted me out of there right away; the constable wanted me locked up with no possibility of bail. They bargained in front of me. The constable referred to my possible involvement in a larger ring of dealers but had no substantiating evidence to prove this accusation. He said that if they let me out, I would be back on the streets where I had been living before they had caught me.

The justice decided that if I could post bail and get myself a place to live and a job, I could be released that night. I was once again given access to a telephone, so I called my friend and told him the amount of bail money I needed. He said he would send it to the station with Tara. I then called Tara and asked if I could stay with her so that I would have a fixed address when I got out. She said yes. Finally, I called Suzie and told her I needed to have work lined up to be released from jail. She said I could start work the next day.

An hour later Tara walked into the police station with the money. It struck me how innocent she looked, with her doe eyes and long blond hair. She handed the money to the police chief so he could count it. I was given the fleece jacket and water bottle I had arrived with, and my heart danced as Tara escorted me out of the station. The justice of the peace was satisfied with the terms, the constable was infuriated that his little mouse had been set free, and I was ecstatic to be walking out into the full-moon night.

One condition of the terms of my release was that I could not leave town. In order to prove my obedience, I had to show up at the station every morning at 8 a.m. sharp to sign in. And every morning the police chief brought me into his office to question me and try to procure some relevant information. He told me that I would get off scot-free if only I would divulge who had sold me my drugs. "No one will ever know," he promised, "and you'll walk away as if nothing ever happened."

But no matter how often he tried this line of reasoning, it didn't work. "I'll know," I told him every time I was asked. "And I won't be able to live with myself."

One morning he made me an offer: I could work for them. "You could come over to the light side," he began. "We'll set you up in a new town, get you an apartment and a new car. You'll be perfect for the job."

I felt like I was in the twilight zone. "I couldn't do that type of work," I replied. "I would have to trick people. And besides, I'm not sure which side represents the light."

The elation I felt on getting out of jail did not last long. I might have regained my physical freedom, but I had a serious court case looming on the horizon. I didn't know anyone who had been caught trafficking who did not do some time in prison. The thought of losing my freedom again—this time for a longer period—was difficult to handle. There was no escape; I was obsessed with the upcoming trial and could find no peace. I grew more paranoid by the day as I convinced myself that I had been set up. I wouldn't speak to anyone, wave, or say hello when I saw them in the streets. The world had again become my enemy, along with everybody in it. My relationship with Paul moved into increasingly fragile territory, and we fought more than ever. I wouldn't go into bars anymore, so we regularly drove out to parking lots far enough from town that there would be no chance of running into anybody. I discovered I could relax if I drank enough red wine and smoked enough Drum cigarettes before going to sleep. My anxiety was so high that my depressions gave way to an almost constant mania.

I found a good lawyer who seemed to care about more than the amount of money she would be making from my case, and I had friends who'd been in similar trouble and could counsel me. I could not go directly to Jay, for obvious reasons, but I knew from mutual acquaintances that he was keeping tabs on the situation. I was eventually allowed to leave town for short periods, but only if I told the cops where I was headed and how long I would be gone. When I arrived at my destination, I had to go to the local police department, which would have already been contacted by the Jasper detachment, and sign in once each week.

As I was not functioning very well within the confines of either town or society, Paul and I went to the mountains every chance we got. I was freaked at the prospect of going to prison and often thought about running away to Alaska. But we realized that a life like that would have its own stresses, and there would be no conceivable end to its duration.

On my lawyer's advice, I decided to plead not guilty for reasons of entrapment, and elected trial by judge and jury. Canada did not have laws against entrapment at the time, but the United States did, and my lawyer felt this was my best chance of getting off without doing time.

The court kept pushing my trial date back. Although I did not know it at the time, the man I had sold the drugs to was one of Canada's top narcotics officers, and the authorities were not at all happy that he would be showing up in court to testify in my two-bit case. They knew that gangs like the Hells Angels regularly sent artists into courtrooms to draw accurate portraits of undercover narcs. This would blow the cover of a highly trained specialist.

And so it went for five months, during which time I had to make several court appearances. Finally, on the morning of August 18, I was waiting in a room at the courthouse, stressed and angry at how long this was taking, when my lawyer came into the room and told me the deal.

"I've just been in a meeting with the crown prosecutor and the judge," she said, "and they told me that if you walk into that courtroom today and plead guilty, they will let you off with a fine, probation, and a criminal record, but no prison term."

I felt like I was in a movie. I could not believe that our justice system was a deal-brokering game. "What about the entrapment angle?" I asked her. "Do we still have a chance with that?"

She looked me straight in the eyes, as tired of my case as I was. "Yes, we can still go for that, but look what this has cost you already. Not just in terms of money, but the stress. This deal is a sure thing. The entrapment angle is a risk."

"So you think I should accept this offer?" I asked again.

"Yes, that would be my advice to you," she replied.

I stood up and told her I would accept it, and together we walked into the courtroom, where we went through the motions of a hearing. Everything went as promised. The crown prosecutor got up and said his piece, and my lawyer got up and said hers. The judge pronounced the verdict, and it was exactly as we discussed: fine, probation, and a criminal record. I gave no thought to how this record might affect my future; all I knew was that I was free to walk out of the courthouse and restart my life.

Paul was waiting for me in the park, relieved that I had not been taken away and locked up. I told him about the deal and how much the fine was, and I set to work with Suzie to earn enough to pay the fine and also build up savings so I could focus exclusively on ice climbing over the winter. Now that the case was behind me and the summer was almost over, I thought of nothing but the plethora of climbs before me.

Paul and I began gearing up for another winter of climbing on the Icefields Parkway. This would be our second winter living in the truck, and though I didn't mind the time we spent living on the parkway, I no longer wanted to stay in my truck when I was in town. I had been woken up too many times by the wardens telling me that I couldn't spend the night wherever I happened to be parked, that I had to move along. They knew my truck and they knew us, and the anonymous days of sleeping in parking lots were coming to an end. I moved into an apartment building at the east end of town, renting a bachelor suite. This was the perfect place to return to each weekend to sort gear, bake bread, and make granola bars for our next foray down the parkway.

Even though Paul had brought a positive new dimension to my life in the form of climbing, he had also brought an increasingly negative aspect. I was no stranger to violence, either my own or other people's, but with Paul it had become a frequent and permanent part of our relationship.

Partway through the winter, Paul was helping his brother in Hinton do some work on a log home. I had spent the day baking, sorting gear, and sharpening our picks and ice screws. When it started to get late, I wondered if Paul was going to return that night. But I had no telephone, and there was no way to find out what was happening.

Finally Paul arrived. When he walked in the door, I saw that his long blond hair, which he almost always wore in a ponytail, had been cut to shoulder length, and he had bangs. This was so out of character for him that I was startled. I asked him why he'd decided to get his hair cut and who had cut it for him.

"None of your goddamned business!" he yelled at me, and I knew he had been out drinking.

I had gotten used to his outbursts of rage; they were always waiting beneath the surface and were triggered by seemingly trivial things. I told him that I was just curious, that it was shocking for him to come home with a completely different haircut, especially since he had mentioned nothing about it.

"Are you accusing me of cheating on you?"

He was yelling so loudly I was worried someone would call the cops. I told him this.

"Fuck you. Who are you, telling *me* to be careful about involving cops in our lives?"

I sensed that we were on more dangerous ground than usual. We were not outside, in a truck, where I could drive away. We were in an apartment building and were surrounded by other tenants who could hear what was going on.

"You fucking cunt; you stupid little whore. How dare you accuse me of anything when you were just a wandering drug dealer when I met you!"

He was coming at me now, and I tried to back away. He caught me by the scruff of the neck and threw me onto the kitchen floor. He was still yelling at me while he kicked me and punched me, over and over. I thought I was going to die, that this time he was going to kill me. I screamed loudly, hoping that someone next door would hear me and come over or call the cops.

I'll never know if he let me escape on purpose or if I fought back enough in my adrenaline-infused terror to get away, but the next thing I knew I was pounding on the neighbours' door, screaming and crying. They let me in, and I realized that not only were they having a social gathering, but my torso was half naked. I tried to wrap my shirt around me, but it was so torn it was virtually impossible to pull together. Everyone was stunned, and no one knew how to deal with me. I was sobbing uncontrollably in between periods of hysteria. Finally a woman came over with a shirt and told me to put it over my ripped one. Then she asked me if I wanted her to call the cops.

She couldn't have known what a terrifying suggestion this was. I said no, that I just needed to make sure Paul was gone so I could go back into my apartment and figure out what to do next. She and her boyfriend accompanied me back down the hall, and it was clear that Paul had left the building. The door to my apartment was wide open. Everything inside the room had been smashed and strewn around. I assured the couple that I was okay, and I thanked them. It was awkward, but I was in no state to worry about that at the time.

I changed my shirt and looked in the mirror. I had a black eye, and my lower back hurt like hell. I turned around and saw that there were large bruises around the area of my kidneys. The toes on my left foot felt broken. I couldn't stay in the apartment because Paul had a key. I grabbed my jacket and my truck keys, locked the door, and drove over to Gunner's place.

When I came through the door, he knew exactly what had happened: this was not the first time he had watched me go through this with Paul. He gave me a hug and made me some strong coffee. We sat at his kitchen table for a long time, looking at each other but not saying much.

"What will you do now?' he asked.

I felt awkward. I knew there shouldn't be any question in my mind about what to do. But I didn't answer him. I felt lost and alone. After what felt like a long time, Gunner made me a makeshift bed on his couch, and we called it a night. Within days I had taken a construction job; manual labour had always been my refuge when I needed some structure in my life.

I told Paul I didn't want to go climbing with him anymore. Our recent fight was not the first time he had beaten me up, and although I didn't leave him, neither did I trust him. He took off by himself, doing solo climbs of waterfall ice and alpine peaks. He would be gone for a few days at a time and stay with me for the remaining days of the week. Our relationship remained intense, alternating between violent fights and passionate sex, sometimes in the same hour. I felt trapped. I believed that I loved him but could not reconcile that with the constant threat of violence.

Eventually Paul was offered work with a log-house builder out of Hinton and moved into a small cabin on the job site. I gave notice to my landlord and moved out of my apartment and back into my truck. I had met other ice climbers at this point and now spent several days each week out on frozen waterfalls. I visited Paul on my days off from climbing.

It was during one of these visits that I made a life-altering decision.

I was sipping coffee in the warmth of the cabin after Paul had gone off to work. I was trying to read a book, but no matter how hard I tried I couldn't concentrate on the words. I had been feeling particularly angry and confused. Looking around the room, I made a split-second decision and picked up every single thing I owned. I stuffed it all into the knapsack I carried with me wherever I went, took it outside, and dropped it in the passenger seat of my truck. I walked over to Paul's job site and told him I was going into Hinton to pick up some groceries. I drove the quarter mile out to the highway. When I reached it, instead of turning left into town, I turned right and headed south toward Lake Louise.

Two months before my final hearing, Paul and I had driven to Canmore to climb the northeast ridge of Ha Ling Peak and some other routes on Yamnuska, a bluff on the First Nations reserve near Exshaw. Now I had decided I would move to Canmore and apply for a Parks Canada job in Banff. Up to this moment I had thought I'd never leave Jasper, that it was the most beautiful place in the world, with mountains and drugs and everything I could possibly want or need. But I had started to feel boxed in. I already had a reputation for being wild, for ruining my life and my brain with drugs, and now I had a criminal record to boot. As those last months went by, I felt more and more that I had to get out of that little mountain town and away from my unhealthy alliance with Paul.

I was excited by my decision because I knew it would be a fresh start in a place where nobody knew anything about me or my past. It was my chance to make a complete and final break with drugs and drug dealing.

11

EAST OF EDEN

CANMORE WAS ONCE A LITTLE-KNOWN MINING TOWN off the Trans-Canada Highway between Calgary and Banff, with a population about the same size as Jasper's. Hosting the Nordic skiing events during the 1988 Calgary Winter Olympics put it on the map, and the town soon became one of the premier winter-sports destinations in North America. By the time I moved there in February 1994, the population had jumped from four thousand to six thousand and the recreational real estate boom was just getting underway. Because of Canmore's large climbing population, there were more local rock-climbing areas here, as well as more potential climbing partners, than at any other place in Canada. Guiding was the biggest business outside of construction, and the area was a world-class ice-climbing destination in winter.

For the time being, though, I needed a job. Richard Bremner had a construction company based in Canmore. He had a reputation for being brusque, but I respected the way he had run a project I worked on in Jasper, and I liked the guys I had met on his crew.

"What do you want?" he demanded when he saw me standing in the doorway to his office.

"Work," I replied.

He sat back in his chair, looking down at the papers on his desk. After a few moments he looked up at me: "When do you want to start?"

I said I could start the following morning or any time after that.

"Tomorrow morning, then. Be here at 6:30 sharp."

I went downtown to a pay phone and called Wendy, a woman I knew from Jasper who had moved to Canmore the previous year, to see if she could suggest where I might rent a room until spring.

"You're in luck," she said. "My landlord just left for Nepal, and there's an empty bedroom you can move into."

Within ten minutes, Wendy and I were hauling my duffel bags into the condo. She cooked dinner that night and told me about her life since moving to Canmore. She commended me on getting away from Jasper and told me that she had never looked back. I hoped I would be able to say the same thing someday.

I started work the next day, laying underground water and sewer pipes in Lake Louise. We left town at 6:30 in the morning and returned around the same time at night. I was soon following a routine in which I would get home from work, draw a hot bath, have dinner with a glass of wine, and go to bed. But after working for thirty-five days straight, I needed a break. I asked the foreman for a day off. He looked at me like I was crazy, so I went into Bremner's office.

"What do you want?" he asked in his usual tone of voice.

"A day off," I replied. "I haven't had one since I started working for you over a month ago."

He looked at me as if he couldn't believe I could be so demanding. "So, you want to be on the drunk list?"

I must have looked confused, because he explained that every second Friday, when I got paid, I could take the weekend off. Who knew?

My first winter in Canmore flew by on this new schedule, and then my roommate hooked me up with a new climbing partner.

Wendy was friends with Pat Morrow, a photographer and filmmaker from the area, who told her he needed a belayer for an upcoming photo shoot on Louise Falls with the well-known American ice climber Joe Josephson. Wendy suggested he should have a chick in the photo shoot and offered my services for the day, so that weekend I drove out to Lake Louise and went ice climbing for the first time since arriving in town. We had a fun day out and stopped to eat dinner on our way home. This was when

I discovered that Joe had been kicked out of Canada by the immigration authorities and had until March to leave. He and Pat joked that he needed to find a wife in order to stay. Only half jokingly, I said that if he couldn't find anyone else, I would consider it.

Joe got in touch with me often during the remainder of the winter. He was writing a new edition of *Waterfall Ice*, the Canadian Rockies ice-climbing guide, and we went out every weekend to climb routes he was not familiar with so that he could check on the accuracy of his information.

When spring arrived I left my construction job and moved out of my room at Wendy's and back into my truck. I rock climbed whenever the weather was good. I also applied for, and obtained, a job with Parks Canada on the Banff trail crew. But it wasn't as straightforward as I had thought it would be.

When I went for the interview in May, shortly after moving out of Wendy's, I was given a sheaf of forms to fill out. I noticed that one of the forms granted permission to do a criminal record check. I signed the form and thought nothing further of it; after all, I was going to be living in the bush, running chainsaws all day. Who would care about a minor transgression in my past?

It turned out that many people cared about criminal records. A week after I was told I had been accepted for the position, I got a call from the parks service. My criminal record check had revealed my conviction in Jasper, so I was ordered to come to the information centre in Banff to have my fingerprints taken. I couldn't figure out why they would want my fingerprints again—the cops already had them—but I showed up to do as they wished. The woman behind the desk treated me like a degenerate and brusquely took me through the fingerprinting regimen.

Since I had told many people that I had a job, I began worrying about how I would explain this sudden turn of events if it now turned out I did not have one.

The women in Parks Canada's head office and in the information centre tried to block me from getting the job. They argued that I was a criminal who could not be trusted and who might steal things from the wardens' cabins if they gave me the job. I called up Don, the man who had interviewed me, and gave him an abridged account of what had happened in

Jasper and how I had ended up with my criminal record. He went to bat for me and personally vouched for my integrity. He told the objectors that he would take full responsibility for my actions while I was employed by the parks service. I was extremely grateful that he did this for me—he could just as easily have hired the next person on the list. His response when I admitted my past to him was direct: "I believe everyone deserves a second chance." So for ten days at a time I would be living and working in the bush. Then I would get four days off to come back to town and live in my truck.

Meanwhile, Joe had moved back to Montana. He came up about once a month and we would go into the mountains to climb together. As time went on, though, it was harder and harder for Joe to come back into Canada. I couldn't cross the border because of my criminal record, so we decided to get married. We timed our wedding for the first weekend in November, the same weekend as the Banff Mountain Film Festival, and invited only our close friends and Joe's family to the ceremony, which was held in the home of a photographer friend and officiated by a justice of the peace. And then we moved into a rented house, a tiny miner's cabin in the oldest section of Canmore, and began our life together.

Joe was very different from the other men in my life, and this is precisely what had attracted me to him. He was predictable, had not experienced the highs and lows I was all too familiar with, and he had a stabilizing influence on me. He drank socially but didn't do any drugs, and neither did any of his friends. We were good friends and climbing partners, and that was what I needed at the time. I was still experiencing depressions, and although dealing with them was just as difficult as ever, I had resigned myself to the fact that there was nothing I could do except continue coping.

A few months after the wedding we were invited to dinner by Barry Blanchard, a mountain guide and Canada's best-known alpinist. I had known Barry since I started to ice climb, as Paul and I would run into him on the Icefields Parkway from time to time. He had just returned from a guiding job on Mount Everest, where he had met his future wife, Catherine. She had recently moved to Canmore to be with him.

As Joe and I pulled up to Barry's place, I caught sight of a beautiful brunette standing in the doorway. Wearing jeans, a white cotton shirt, and cowboy boots, she looked to me like she had walked straight out of a movie set. During dinner I discovered she had been living in Boston and had some experience in film, which was how she wound up on Mount Everest—as an assistant to mountaineer-filmmaker David Breashears. Catherine was articulate and funny, and we hit it off instantly. She had read more books than anyone I knew, could come up with quotes from movies that fit perfectly into every conversation, and was a great cook—she had put together a fantastic Mexican meal for us.

After dinner, Catherine and I went into the kitchen to mix some cocktails, and she asked if I had met Karen, "the Kiwi woman who just moved here to climb ice." I told her I hadn't, so the next morning Catherine and I walked over to the Coffee Mine, where Karen worked. When we came through the door, Catherine pointed Karen out: curly black hair, pale freckled skin, and about my height. We walked over to the counter, where Karen recognized Catherine and said hello. Catherine simply replied, "Karen, this is Margo, another woman ice climber in the valley. I thought you two should meet." Karen and I exchanged a few words, but there were people behind us who needed to be served, so we arranged to meet that evening and go for a walk.

I picked Karen up after she got off work. We drove down to the Bow River, which has a great trail system where we could walk and talk. I sensed that she was shy, at least compared with me, so I just started talking about whatever came into my mind. "Why did you move over here?" I asked. "Don't you have beautiful mountains in New Zealand?"

Karen replied, "We have mountains, but we don't have the steep terrain and waterfall ice you have over here. That's what I came here to climb."

She was not very talkative that night, but I had no trouble picking up the slack. I found myself confessing many things I would not have told most people. I will never know whether she was too intrigued by my confessions or too shy to verbalize her most cherished beliefs about the world and its misfortunes. Whatever the case, I walked away from that evening with a sense that I had laid bare my feelings and thoughts but had learned nothing about my newly acquired friend. That would soon change.

It was late enough in the fall for the ice-climbing season to be getting underway. Karen and I made plans to go out the following week and see what adventure would find us. We decided to go to Ranger Creek and climb a waterfall called R&D, in Kananaskis Country. I picked Karen up at 7 a.m. sharp, and we began the forty-five-minute drive to the parking lot on the Smith-Dorrien Highway.

"Do you think it's okay to date your boss?" Karen asked shortly after we pulled out of town. She had a huge crush on Brad, the co-owner of the Coffee Mine. "I go in the back, where he bakes, as often as I can. Sometimes when it's not busy he lets me help him."

I asked her if she could get me the recipe for the chocolate banana bread that had become my favourite climbing snack.

"He's so cute, but he's so shy I don't know if he'll ever ask me out," she persisted.

"Then you'll have to take the bull by the horns," I said. She wasn't sure if she could muster the courage for that, but I assured her she could. "What else are you going to do—work with him for the next two years and have nothing happen because you're both too shy to break the ice?"

We parked the truck at the trailhead, finished packing our packs, and grabbed our ski poles for the hike in to the climb. We had been hiking for only a few minutes when Karen started asking me about my relationship with Joe. "What's it like climbing with Joe? He's such a good climber, you must feel like you're following him around most of the time."

It was true. I had been ice climbing at a decent level when I met him, but we usually went out on really hard climbs together, and Joe was way faster than me on lead. "Yeah, it's a bit of a problem," I agreed. "It's easy to feel like a shitty climber when your partner and his friends are that good."

Karen told me about a book she had read by Arlene Blum, who said that the best way for a woman to become a better climber was to climb with other women. That was what Karen wanted to do, and she counselled me to do the same.

"Well," I replied, "that'll be a lot easier now that I've found you."

After forty minutes of walking uphill we were at the base of the route. R&D is a beautiful one-pitch climb with a grade that can be challenging early in the season, which is the only time people climb it. It is in a tight valley with slopes angling down toward the approach gully from all sides, so it is climbed before this terrain gets too heavily loaded with snow and the avalanche hazard becomes too high. This was a good year; it had been cold for weeks now, so there was lots of ice, but there had been little snow. We geared up at the base, just off to the right of the climb. Karen and I talked the entire time; in fact, we had not stopped talking since I had picked her up two hours earlier. It seemed as though we had embarked on a never-ending conversation, such was our delight in each other's company.

Karen offered me the lead. I racked my ice screws on my harness and gear loop while Karen flaked out the ropes. I preferred to climb with a two-rope system so that I always had a means to rappel without trailing a separate line. I tied into one end of each of the ropes, and as soon as Karen had me on belay I started up.

"Good job, Margo," she said as I was placing my first screw. I was pleased and surprised, because I had never been complimented on my ice climbing before. I felt supported, as if my lead meant as much to Karen as her own would have. I looked down at her and smiled as I clipped the ropes into my first piece of protection, then put my gloved hand back into my leash and continued up the ice.

As I progressed toward the top of the climb, I felt great relief to be climbing with another woman. Most of my male partners were not very supportive of me, especially not of my leading. They wanted to do the leads themselves and maintained they were faster and that it was more efficient to do it that way. I had started to feel like a belay slave rather than an equal partner, and it was not doing anything to improve my climbing.

When I got to the top I clipped into the two-bolt anchor that had been drilled in by some previous party. I brought in the remaining rope and yelled down to Karen that she was on belay. Within minutes she began to climb. I stood at the top feeding the rope through my belay device, happy to be in a new place, away from my life of drugs—and to have found a woman who shared my passion for ice climbing after three years of climbing exclusively with men. With Karen I found encouragement to flourish while exercising my own athletic abilities. I was physically very strong, much stronger than most of the women I had known in my life, but I had fears and trepidations with roots that stretched as far back as I could remember. These hampered me in climbing and in life, and it was these fears that Karen picked up on in our first forays onto the frozen world of waterfall ice. Karen had an intrinsic understanding of my fears, and an equal amount of spontaneous support for the power and potential that she saw beneath them. Her presence was her gift, and in this presence I found a sense of safety that I had yearned for but had never experienced with anyone.

After that, we climbed together as often as possible. All our money and spare time went into our passion. In the evenings after our climbs we sat, drank red wine, and talked about our lives. I would tweak any equipment that needed it, mainly my ice picks and screws. Karen would sharpen her picks but let me take care of her screws. I had been sharpening my work tools all my life, and this had given me a steady hand and keen eye for perfect angles.

"Well, have you jumped Brad yet?" I asked her one night as I pushed my file over the metal surfaces.

Karen's face turned a deep crimson and broke into a mischievous grin. We both burst out laughing at her obvious response to my question. Karen proceeded to tell me about the day she had asked Brad out on a date, how it had all happened while they were baking muffins in the kitchen of the café, and how they had gone to the bar at the Sherwood House after work that very evening for a few drinks.

"So," Karen concluded, "it's a done deal. We've been dating for a few weeks now, and it's wonderful."

Karen wanted to be a sponsored climber. Not only was it an exotic and exciting lifestyle to her but it was also a means to fund her chosen dreams and sustain them. She and Brad had started dating just months before she was due to head out on one of her earliest expeditions, an all-women ascent of Cho Oyu in Nepal.

I had no interest in going on expeditions. I did not feel stable enough to travel and put myself in new environments with new people. Although I had quit doing drugs, I still had no control over the huge swings in my moods. Besides, there was so much to do right here in the Canadian Rockies; it was not like I would be missing out. One of the things that was helping me in my new life was the introduction of routine, and I didn't want to be away from this for more than a few days at a time. I had only recently begun sleeping through the night after being plagued by insomnia for as long as I could remember.

In my new life with Joe, I had found that the more predictable I could keep my outer circumstances, the less chaotic was my inner state. I also realized that the reason I had felt stable in my life with Jay was precisely because he had taken control of everything—much as my mother had done. With Joe, who was the opposite of this and did not try to control me, I was learning to create the stability I needed in an entirely new way.

12

RACING WITH SHADOWS

In late February 1995, I was convalescing from an accident that had caused my left arm and leg to swell to twice their normal size. A huge chunk of ice had fallen on me while I was climbing Expert's Choice with Brad Wrobleski, a photographer friend who often accompanied Joe and me on climbs. It was the closest call I had ever had in the mountains, and I was lucky I was not more badly injured. I could barely walk for the first month and spent every day alone in the house while Joe went out climbing. Physical activity had become my sole way of dealing with depression since quitting drugs, and now I had lost this outlet. As the weeks went by, my mental state deteriorated. I knew I needed a positive focus to help me get through this period.

I decided to start my own company, Wild Orchid Landscaping. When Joe told his parents about the idea, they sent me two thousand dollars toward my goal. I never wanted to be questioned about my past again, as the parks service had done, and running my own company seemed like the perfect solution. I also knew that working for myself was the only way to navigate my depressions successfully; their arrival was impossible to predict, and they were gaining a stronger hold on me as I moved into my thirties.

I resumed working for Bremner, who let me work four days a week so that I could build up my landscaping business the rest of the time. He also gave Karen work during the summer months. I was thrilled to have another woman on the job site, which until now had been exclusively male, and Karen and I were able to spend more time together as a result of this new development.

My summer was filled with activity. Bremner had landed a contract to build the large-animal overpasses on the highway between Banff and Lake Louise, and when I wasn't busy there I worked on pamphlets and other marketing ideas for my company. In every spare moment, Karen and I went rock climbing. In this way I kept myself so busy that before I knew it the summer had flown by in a flurry of activity. Throughout the fall I dreamt of climbing frozen waterfalls. Karen and I had a "hit list" of climbs we wanted to do together, and we systematically ticked off two of these every weekend during the winter.

In February 1996, fifteen months into my marriage to Joe, Karen and I were on Murchison Falls, a classic grade 5 waterfall on the Icefields Parkway. I had not been doing well lately; I was psychologically defeated by my depressions, which if anything were getting longer and deeper. I had thought that giving up drugs would solve, or at least alleviate, the problem, but two years after winning the struggle to overcome my addiction, my underlying demons were resurfacing in all their destructive savagery.

There is a little approach pitch to Murchison, short, at a low angle, and easy enough for a climber with any experience to solo. I was partway up this pitch when I leaned into my axes and began to sob into the ice. I was not on the ice anymore; I was lost in the emotions that had begun to take over my life.

I could hear Karen's voice coming from below, a soft and gentle chain of words telling me to stay where I was, to go no higher, that she was about to come up and stand beside me and help me get back down to the safety of flat snow. I barely heard her; overwhelming emotions pounded in my blood and body. But the next thing I knew she was there right beside me, standing on the front points of her crampons with her axes in the ice, telling me that we were going to climb back down the ice together. All I could think was, "But we've driven all this way. We're here to go climbing!"

"We're not going to climb today," Karen replied. "We're going to go back to Canmore and figure out what we need to do to stabilize your emotional state so you can function again."

I surrendered to her logic and climbed down the section of ice that I had gone up. We were silent as we took off our crampons and harnesses, loosened the laces of our boots, and stuffed gear into our packs for the hike back out to the road. I felt like a ghost, as though I couldn't quite figure out how to inhabit my body, or my life. As though I didn't know who I was or what I wanted in my life. I felt empty to the point where it scared me, and I kept trying unsuccessfully to either fill the void or run away from myself.

As I voiced these feelings, Karen said, "It scares me too. That's why getting to the bottom of this is the most important thing for you to focus on right now."

After the episode on Murchison, I decided the safest thing to do was quit ice climbing for the season and resume climbing only when I felt more stable. I went back to work for Bremner, slipping in and out of depression for the remainder of the winter. My marriage to Joe was friendly and peaceful, but I longed for more passion. He was wrapped up in his climbing career, and we hadn't done much of anything together. When spring arrived I kept myself busy with Wild Orchid, construction work, and, when the weather was good enough, my rock-climbing weekends with Karen. Although this schedule kept me on an even keel, I wasn't doing anything more to address the underlying problem. I was at a loss, as the only advice I got, wherever I turned, was to go on the antidepressant drugs that I was still being offered by mental health practitioners.

This schedule carried me through the summer until it was once again time to get excited about the climbs Karen and I had planned for the upcoming winter. We talked about my marriage a lot that year. She didn't understand why I didn't just up and leave Joe. I admitted to her that I was terrified my life would become unstable again if I was not with him, and this was the last thing in the world I wanted to risk. She replied that I, not Joe, deserved credit for creating a stable life for myself, and she pointed out that there was no good reason to stay in an unhappy marriage.

My need for passion was becoming overwhelming, and when I went back to working in construction full time in the fall, I ended up having an affair with one of my co-workers. The winter went by much as the previous winter had done, with work and ice climbing. I began spending more time in the bar with the guys after work, as I didn't like being at home in the empty gulf that my marriage to Joe had become. I kept a close eye on my drinking, allowing myself to have only a few beers at a time, but I was keenly aware of the link between my unhappiness at home and the resumption of one of my old habits.

In February 1998, Louis-Julien Roy, a fellow climber and friend, asked if I would like to help out with an ice-climbing festival that he and his employer, Mike Meilicke, the owner of a local climbing-gear store, were putting on that winter. I eagerly accepted the offer. I had enough time to spare, and I saw the festival as a fun social event, something I still enjoyed when not suffering from bouts of depression. Over the next few weeks I pitched in whenever I could, helping to build the ice tower in the middle of town and organize the women's ice-climbing clinics. The event was going to be held over a weekend in March, with speed-climbing competitions on Saturday and the clinics on Sunday.

I had never speed climbed, so I enlisted whoever I could find to come out to Haffner Creek, the local ice-climbing crag, and do laps on the pillars with me. Karen was working a lot that winter and had far less time than I did for both the festival and ice climbing. The competition was a blast, but I realized that I would need to train harder if I was going to be any good at speed climbing. The next day I went back to Haffner Creek with the women who had signed up for the climbing clinic. I felt so much joy in introducing them to the activity that had become the greatest passion in my life. Mike showered me with shwag—gear that had been donated for the event—to show his appreciation, and I told him that I'd had so much fun I wanted to be more involved with the festival the following year.

A few months after the festival, I decided to apply for a pardon for my drug conviction. When I had been convicted, I was told that I would have to wait five years before I applied, and now it was nine months past that anniversary. I had to get the Jasper and Canmore RCMP to fill out forms, as well as complete several documents myself with personal information on my life since the conviction. When all the material was compiled, I put it in an envelope and sent it by registered mail to the National Parole Board in Ottawa.

By this time, the affair with my co-worker had petered out and I had begun sleeping with another man. I knew that I could not continue like this forever and that a decision had to be made. On March 24, 1998, three days shy of my thirty-fourth birthday, I walked into Karen's apartment at noon with a bottle of red wine in my hand. "Today's the day," I announced as I came into the kitchen. She knew exactly what I was talking about; she opened the bottle and poured each of us a glass of wine. We toasted my decision and talked about our lives and our climbing goals for the upcoming year. By late afternoon I was ready to announce my decision to Joe.

Joe was not surprised. He admitted that he knew our relationship would cave in sooner or later. While it was true that I was not getting any support from him for my climbing or my psychological state, I can't imagine how hard it must have been for him to watch me descend into the depths of depression for months at a time and feel powerless to do anything about it.

It was a peaceful breakup, and to mark it we invited twenty friends to a party. In the middle of the festivities we asked them to come into the living room so we could make an announcement. They probably weren't expecting this one: "We're getting a divorce, and we want you all to know that you don't have to get weird about it, that you can invite both of us to parties, because we'll still be friends."

Quite a few jaws dropped, but one of our friends quickly recovered. He smiled and said, "Hey, everybody, Margo's single again!" We all burst out laughing and went back to our drinks and conversations.

13

FEARFUL SYMMETRY

I HAD A STRING OF CASUAL AFFAIRS after my divorce, but I was determined to stay single and work on my personal issues as well as my climbing goals. My landscaping business took off that summer, and now Karen was working for me. We were spending inordinate amounts of time together, working and climbing. I would lie low during my depressions, seeing only Karen, but whenever I came out of them I would make up for my isolation with my partying and socializing. I was drinking moderately but hadn't done drugs in over four years. Most people in my circle knew nothing about my past or my depressions, and I preferred it that way.

When I asked Karen if she had ever been depressed, she promptly answered no. I had consulted several mental health professionals before I reached thirty and knew that the average person had difficulty understanding depression. I wondered what it was about Karen that allowed her to tune in to such a foreign state without any prior experience of it. But I quickly left this train of thought and simply appreciated her support and understanding as I focused on my pain.

Getting to the bottom of a debilitating psychological state is hard work, and it garners no recognition or applause. I watched as my peers held court with their assortment of climbing-related injuries and wondered if the day would come when society would give similar attention to those who suffered invisibly. In the same way, whenever I have had an injury,

I've remarked to myself how wonderful it would be if emotional wounds would obey timelines for healing as, say, a fractured fibula does. How I would have loved to be able to go to a doctor and have her X-ray my heart and say, "Just two more weeks, Ms. Talbot, and you'll never even know you were injured."

But over the past few years I had become more of a realist. I had come to understand that depression was an internal struggle on an invisible battlefield, experienced by an individual alone and perhaps witnessed by loved ones and whatever higher power the depressed person happened to rely on to get through it. So while my physically injured peers were being taken out to luncheons and showered with books and gifts to keep them busy in their convalescence, I hunkered down for another solo journey into the depths of my own psychic hell.

There were brighter days too. During that summer, Karen and I started having more fun in our relationship. We would go to the local fabric shop, buy outrageous pieces of fleece fabric, and sew them around the collar and cuffs of our jean jackets. We went to the Saan store regularly and bought cheap sparkle jewellery and glitter makeup. My life had become more balanced—although I was experiencing deep depressions, I was also experiencing episodes of lightness and fun, which were completely new to me.

Wild Orchid had a banner season. I had more work coming in than I knew what to do with. I hired some of my climber friends, and when they needed time to go into the mountains I would simply hire another friend. I worked every day that summer, putting in beautiful new landscapes, as well as doing maintenance on dozens of existing ones. I would often work ten-hour days and afterward go out for runs or to lift weights at the Nordic Centre gym. I was stronger than I had ever been and had a seemingly endless amount of energy. When I got home at night, I would make dinner and do paperwork until bedtime.

For the first time since I'd started my company, I had enough money saved by autumn to get me through the winter. This meant I did not need to work in construction, so I was able to put all my energy into ice climbing. I went out at every opportunity, climbing an average of four days each week. Although Karen was still my main partner, there were now a handful of women I could go climbing with. I also had a lot of friends, mainly people

I had met in the climbing community. I was still battling depression and anxiety attacks, but the quality of my life was much better.

I think climbing kept me sane. It had become a form of meditation, a place where I could be so focused that the battles inside my psyche faded into the background. I became present in ways that I had never been in any other part of my life. I was addicted to this feeling of complete absorption, and it kept me grounded and centred in the rest of my life. It also allowed me to belong to a community for the first time in my life, and this feeling of validation and belonging was a boost to my confidence level. I had not gotten much support in my life, and when I finally experienced it I began to blossom.

For Karen and me, the Canmore Ice Climbing Festival was one of the highlights of our decade-long friendship. When it was time to start organizing the second year of the festival, both Karen and I signed up. It was perfect for us, as we both had enough free time during the winter months to fulfill this obligation. We loved the social aspect—not just the event itself, but the networking leading up to it. And we loved getting out our glitter makeup and jewellery and sewing fake fur onto another jean jacket or fleece top as the annual event approached. We felt like fashion mavericks starring in our own nighttime television series: *The Glitter Girls Go Ice Climbing.*

It was born innocently enough: a business office open after hours, a basic working knowledge of Corel Draw, and the mischievous sensibilities of two grown women retracing their footsteps back to innocence. We spent many fun-filled days and nights designing the posters, pamphlets, and T-shirts for the festival, moving text and company logos to fit into a cohesive whole on the given space of our medium.

On one of these evenings I took my hands off the computer keyboard and turned to Karen. "You know," I said, "we should have our own logo."

Karen stopped what she was doing and looked over at me with a glint in her eye. "What do you think it should be?"

We decided on *The Glitter Girls*, in a pink starry font enclosed in an oval of the same colour. It was created in minutes. We couldn't stop laughing and were already plotting where we would place ourselves amidst the climbing company logos on our poster. Our deadline was the following afternoon, and we knew that even if Mike noticed our logo, he would have little chance of getting changes made so close to the deadline.

The festival was a huge success, and Sunday evening found us at the closing party, which was held at a bar known as Hooligans on the east end of town. Karen and I were decked out in our fake fur and glitter, and the lights were swimming around the dance floor. We had been dancing together all night, and we needed a break, so I went to the bar to get two glasses of water. By the time I returned, Karen was talking with a slim man in the corner of the room. I walked over and she introduced us.

"Margo, this is Chris Strasser. He's here with Mountain Hardwear."

I said hello and exchanged a few words with him, then walked back onto the dance floor because my favourite song, "Billie Jean," was playing. After what seemed like a long time, Karen came back out to dance, and we barely took another break before the party ended.

On the drive home, she told me that Chris was a marketing rep and that he was going to get her hooked up with some product.

"That's great," I told her. "Now you can look hot on the dance floor *and* out in the mountains."

It was 2 a.m., and though we hadn't drunk very much we were extremely tired. I dropped Karen off, went back to my place, and crashed the instant I got in the house.

Karen was going on at least one serious expedition a year now and was away from Canmore at least two months at a time, usually in the spring or fall. She was getting product and also some money from her sponsors and had started climbing regularly with Sue Nott, a woman from Colorado who was sponsored by the same company. We discussed my going along on one of these trips but decided that I was not ready to put that amount of stress on top of the instabilities I was still dealing with. I began climbing more frequently with other partners, and we found ourselves spending more time apart.

In February 1999 I had been single for a year and my psychological state was relatively stable. I was leading the second pitch on Carlsberg Column, a popular grade 5 ice climb in Field, B.C., and I had stopped to place a screw. I noticed a team of climbers waiting on the ledge below and to my right as I moved up the final pitch of ice. I clipped the screw, and when I placed my axe, it slotted into a hole in the ice. I had never liked hooking my tools, preferring to place the axe in the ice, where it felt more secure. I had started to take my pick out when I heard a voice call up from below. "I'd use that placement if I were you. It's good."

I looked down at the owner of the voice. "Well," I replied, "you're not me."

I turned back to the task at hand and continued up the ice. I was climbing with another woman that day, and when we were both at the top we set up our ropes to rappel. When we got back to the ledge, the man with the friendly advice was waiting. He introduced himself as Grant, started chatting with me, and gave me his phone number in case I was ever in need of a climbing partner. I had plenty of climbing partners—but I called him three days later, and we made a plan to go to the Ghost the following week to climb Malignant Mushroom.

It soon became obvious that Grant wanted to date me, but I was gun-shy. Although my marriage to Joe had gone relatively smoothly, all of my other relationships had been hard on me. Getting close to somebody made me feel uncomfortable at best and gave me outright panic attacks at worst. Nevertheless, we climbed together regularly for the next month, and the end of the season found us hiking out from the Sorcerer in the North Ghost. Grant had been making overtures to me for weeks, but I still had some trepidation. We were discussing how late it was, because I had invited people to the house and it was obvious I wouldn't be back in time. I glanced over at Grant as we walked the last mile of the trail. I finally admitted to myself that I liked this man, that he seemed quite nice, and that we did make excellent climbing partners.

When we got back to my place, people were milling around and socializing. We grabbed a beer and joined in the fun. In my absence, someone else had brought out appetizers and whatever other food they could find in the cupboards. I was not very hungry; I was still running on adrenaline. I had also decided to sleep with Grant. Somehow he knew I had made this decision, because when the guests left, he stayed.

We climbed ice together for the rest of the season, drank dark beer, and had lots of great sex. I had never let anyone get this close to me, and it was freaking me out. Deep-seated insecurities were coming to the surface, and I couldn't seem to get a handle on them. I became more and more frightened by the idea that Grant might leave me, and in the process I did everything I could to push him away. My fear of abandonment, which stretched all the way back to my childhood, was now front and centre.

Grant was also very controlling of me and our relationship, and this did nothing to improve the situation. I grew increasingly dependent on him and felt I had lost the precious ground I had gained since my breakup with Joe. He insisted on leading all of the climbs that we did together, and the one area that I had relied on for my self-confidence began to falter.

In June I was collecting the contents of my mailbox when I noticed an official-looking envelope from Ottawa. It had been over a year since I had applied for a pardon, and in that time I had all but forgotten about it. I would even go so far as to say that I thought I didn't care about the outcome of the application. So when I opened the letter and realized that the pardon had been approved, I was surprised by my reaction: right there in the street I burst out crying. I was overcome with joy as I walked back to the house. I knew what this pardon would mean for me: my criminal record would not come up when someone did a search, except under certain circumstances that the authorities deemed to be in the interest of public safety. I also felt redeemed; I had been investigated and was no longer considered a criminal.

Grant and I climbed together a lot that summer, and when autumn came around I had completely given up my space to him. We had developed a dynamic in which I would try to move closer to him and he would respond by moving further away. It felt like he had shut me out of his heart. No matter how hard I tried to get through, he seemed to be living in a glass tower, and I was always on the outside. I felt like a needy child trying to get approval. This dynamic took so much of my energy that it was affecting my emotional state, and not in a good way.

We were sitting on the couch having coffee one morning when Grant announced that he was moving out. I was shocked. I knew we had a huge problem in our relationship, but he had never talked with me about it or even hinted that he was thinking of ending things. I helped him move his belongings down the street, where he had rented a room in a condo where some of his climber friends lived.

I was devastated and fell back into a state of instability and depression that lasted for months. My anxiety about our relationship became worse when that fear turned into the reality of Grant actually leaving me. Then, just as I was stabilizing from this tailspin, he and I got back together and the cycle started all over.

This was by far the most traumatic relationship I had ever had in my life, and in the midst of it I discovered the missing piece of information that made sense of my lifelong fragile emotional state: I started having memories of the sexual abuse I suffered as a child.

At first the information came to me in dreams. Night after night I would awaken from these dreams at the exact same time. I had started meditating as a way to calm myself, and the visions from my dreams began appearing to me while I was in these states. And then one day while I was doing something very ordinary—washing the dishes—I had my first waking memory of the abuse. I was horror-stricken at the reality of what was, and had been, happening to me.

I remembered being raped by a relative when I was seven years old, and I recalled that the violations had been occurring for some years, as well as for some time afterward. Although I tried, I was unable to remember exactly when they had begun. I also recognized that I knew, even then, that there was no point telling my parents about it, so I had kept this a secret from everyone, including myself.

The emotions I felt now were overwhelming. I was nauseous and dizzy, and I thought I was going to faint right there in front of the sink in my Canmore home. I realized that this was the point at which I had lost all faith in the world, the point when something had snapped inside me and I no longer had anything to trust or hope for or believe in.

As soon as this memory emerged, I realized that I had never totally forgotten the violations—I had merely distracted myself from thinking about them for thirty years. And I understood why I had hidden those memories from myself: I'd had to compartmentalize them in order to function in my world as a powerless child. It was a protective mechanism that had gotten me through the worst parts of my life, but it was now hindering my progress. I knew that the memories were surfacing for a reason—so that I could look at them and release them, so that I could heal those parts of my life that had been too painful to look at for the past three decades.

When I told Grant about this, I could tell from the look on his face that he was not keen to sign up for an exploration of this part of my past. I tried explaining it to him: "So many things are starting to make sense for me, Grant, but I'm going to need to get help to sort through it. I need to heal in order for my life, and our relationship, to move forward."

For a minute he said nothing, and I couldn't tell from his facial expression what he was thinking. When he finally spoke, I was stunned by his response.

"I don't believe you can heal from this," he replied. His voice held no emotion; he simply stated it as a matter of fact.

It took a few moments for the significance of what he had just said to sink in. When it finally did, I said, "Well, you'll have to leave then. Because I am going to heal, and I can't do it with someone around who doubts me."

Grant agreed to leave. I was dumbstruck—I felt like I was being abandoned on a sinking ship in the middle of the ocean—and I was deeply disappointed that he had no interest in working through this with me, but I had no choice. I had to face what I had been running from.

When Grant walked out that door, I fell into the abyss that had been waiting for me all my life.

14

RIPTIDE

I WAS CAUTIONED BY MY SISTER JANE to ensure I had a support network in place before venturing into the traumatic experiences of my childhood. I had no idea whether I had the appropriate tools to deal with what I would find inside. I remember walking to the precipice, peering down, and thinking: I can't go there. The leap was too scary and the landing unknown. I wasn't sure how much more I could take. Death might be a welcome end to my pain, as I had no idea when or if it would ever end otherwise. I was charting unknown territory.

Each time I delved into my suppressed memories, the route was familiar until I reached a spot where I'd been only once or twice before. Then came the terror of submerging more deeply. There were no longer any bearings, any signposts: I was adrift in a void. It was so dark and compelling that I forgot to wonder if I could get myself back out again.

One morning I felt like a hollowed-out shell, eerily empty and devoid of hope. For months I had barely been functioning. The hardest thing was waking up and realizing I had to make it through another day. On this morning, birds were chirping outside my window, and I told myself that if they could be so thrilled about the new day, surely I could get out of bed. Yet within hours of comparing myself with the birds, I was calling the suicide crisis hotline.

Everyone knows about these hotlines: you see their phone numbers advertised on the doors of bathroom stalls and in the waiting rooms of doctors and social service agencies. You never think you will be the one to call in—that you will be so desperate, and so lacking in alternatives that you will not only have the number written down on a piece of paper somewhere in your house but that you will actually pick up the phone one day and call it. However, in the spring of my thirty-sixth year, that is exactly what I did. I did not do it with a moment of hesitation but, rather, with a sense of urgency. My mental state was becoming more fragile by the month, and without drugs to numb the pain I was at a complete loss as to how to cope.

A woman with a gentle voice answered the phone. "Hello, my name is Chelsea, and I want you to know that I'm here for you."

I burst out crying as soon as I opened my mouth to speak. "My name is Margo, and I'm trying to figure out why I should carry on."

Chelsea took over the conversation from there. She was obviously well trained to deal with such situations, and although I don't remember exactly what she said, I do remember the influence it had on me. I calmed down, and I had the feeling that things were going to be okay. Chelsea's voice was soothing, and I sensed that she cared about the state I was in.

"Let me give you an address in Calgary," she said as we neared the end of our conversation, "and we can set you up with an appointment tomorrow afternoon, if you can make it."

Not only could I make it; I had nowhere else I would rather go. Nothing meant more to me now than to have someone with whom to share my feelings. I drove into Calgary the following afternoon and felt comforted by the support I received from the women in that office. They walked me through the support systems that were in place for people struggling with issues such as mine, and they encouraged me to stay in touch and to book another appointment whenever I felt the need.

When I told Karen about the meeting, she urged me to make an appointment with a professional. "This is getting too big for me, Margo, and I'm scared for you. You need to get some professional help."

Two days later I was sitting in the office of a clinical social worker, telling her what I had told every mental health practitioner who tried to break into the prison of my psyche: I was not interested in being alive, but this did not mean that I wanted to kill myself. It was crucial to me that they understood this, because it was a fulcrum of my everyday existence. To me, it was normal to feel that ending my life was a viable option, and I wasn't going to talk with any shrink who didn't view this trait in the same way.

Elaine was different from the rest, and I sensed this within minutes of walking into her office. My first instinct on meeting someone was to judge them; it was a defensive reflex that kept people from getting too close to me. But I could feel a connection with her as soon as I moved through this initial reaction. I felt like she understood me completely and knew exactly what I was going through. There was none of the dancing around topics that I had experienced with other professionals: Elaine went straight to the core issues. I had arrived in my work clothes, skinny as a rake and plagued with constant headaches from malnourishment because I could never eat during my lengthy depressions. Although we had scheduled this first appointment in Banff, she told me that all future meetings would take place at her office in Canmore.

"You lack containment," she proclaimed at the beginning of our second session. I had no idea what she was talking about. "Your trauma bleeds into every corner of your reality, touches every moment of every day. You need a ritual for when you allow this to bleed through, and for when you don't. That way you can function for a good part of your life and, when need be, you can open the Pandora's box of your psyche and have a look."

Elaine suggested that I buy a literal Pandora's box with a lid that could be the physical representation of my psyche. When I took it off the shelf and opened it, my trauma could come spilling out for all to see; but when I closed the lid and put it back on the shelf, that would signify to my self that it was time to get on with my "real" life.

I went out with Karen the next day to look for this box to contain my psyche. We found the perfect container, the size of a shoebox and made of thick wood. It had pressed flowers on the top, which was hinged. A railroad spike was attached to each corner, allowing the box to stand on four metal feet. It was beautiful, but it felt like such a frivolous thing to be spending money on. Karen, noticing my hesitation, instantly understood what was going on. "I know you're having trouble with the idea of buying yourself something, but this is really important, Margo. You need to learn to give yourself gifts. I buy myself things all the time."

I knew she was right. Although I did buy myself things, they were all practical and could be used for a specific purpose. I felt silly buying something that was merely a representation of something intangible. As I traced the flowers with my finger, I figured out how to frame this purchase in a way that made it more practical to me.

"I'm giving myself a deadline of two years to move out of my traumatized state," I announced. "I'm tired of living with the constant pain and anxiety, as well as the depression itself. I don't want to become one of those people who sit in Narcotics Anonymous meetings for the rest of their life, calling themselves an addict, chain-smoking cigarettes and downing their fiftieth cup of coffee for the day. Those are symptoms of trauma, no matter how cleverly disguised, and I am going to be free of mine once and for all."

I saw Elaine once a week throughout that fall and winter. She slowly taught me the skills I needed to work through my darkest episodes. In March 2001 I admitted to her that I didn't think I could go on, that I was thinking of ways to end the torment. She stayed calm and stared into my eyes. I continued, telling her how I had wanted to drive off the road on my way to the ski hill the day before, how there was this steep, long embankment on the drive up to Mount Norquay that I wanted to go toppling over, into oblivion. I told her that the main reason I'd stayed on the road was that I was afraid I would fuck it up and end up paralyzed instead of dead. And then I would have a whole new set of problems to deal with.

Elaine said it was important for me to acknowledge these feelings, allow them to move through me, and not feel ashamed of them or embarrassed. She reminded me of my earlier statement that not wanting to be alive did not necessarily translate into committing suicide. "It's the pain you want to end, Margo, not your life." Elaine was the only person besides Karen I could be straight with about this topic. I never saw what the big deal was: some kids grew up and wanted to be millionaires; I wanted to exit the planet in the most painless and least messy way possible.

I sat beside her desk, Kleenex in one hand, pen in the other. Elaine knew that I liked to write, so she made sure I had an implement in my hand to jot down anything that I might not want to share with her. But there was nothing I didn't want to share; I felt understood and accepted every moment I was in her office. She even gave me an after-hours number at which I could reach her, and this gave me a sense of assurance that I needed (although I never once used the privilege).

I believed I could also see myself from Elaine's perspective: a healthy, well-dressed Caucasian woman lost in a maze of despair, tormented by sadness and painful childhood memories. I knew I could never undo the experiences of a whole lifetime, but neither could I allow these experiences to control my world any longer. Margo had to come to the fore and take charge, be the authority in my life that I had never had, and create the safety and peace I sought within.

I felt better after each visit with Elaine, but within days of returning home I would find myself drowning in darkness again. Spring and summer passed in this way, and just when I thought my mental state couldn't get any worse, it did.

I woke up one day to find that the normal cardinal points of my psychic compass were gone; there was nothing to cling to, nothing separating me from psychological annihilation. *Is this what it feels like to go crazy?* I asked myself as the world slipped further and further away from me. There weren't enough books about it, I decided, and I made a vow that if I lived through this experience, I would write one. Sane people have society to tell them what to do, I realized. Crazy people need a manual.

I boiled water to make coffee in my Bodum, the same French press I had used when I was with Jay. Those days now seemed like heaven, blissful and filled with purpose. For the past several weeks I hadn't been able to concentrate on anything: work, climbing, running my daily errands. I could read only a paragraph at a time in a book or magazine, and even then the words didn't make much sense. Powerful emotions had taken over my mind, and it seemed that my logical and analytical abilities had simply evaporated. The way in which I had navigated the world for the past three and a half decades was no longer working for me. I was terrified, and my first thought was that I should never have gone off drugs—whatever damage they had done to me and my life was nothing compared to the breakdowns since I'd quit and now this indefinable netherworld, this no man's land.

When the kettle boiled, I poured the hot water onto the dark coffee grounds that sat in the bottom of the glass jar. I rinsed the plunger with the remaining water from the kettle and placed it on top, the handle sticking up. I put a small saucepan of soy milk on the stove and began heating this up. I noticed I was naked, which wasn't odd for me, but I felt I needed a layer of insulation between me and the world, a buffer zone. I found my faded Levis, a white cotton shirt, and my jean jacket. Then I went to the back porch and slipped my cowboy boots over my calves. I felt better, even though I knew this veneer of separation from the world was nothing but a Band-Aid on a gaping wound.

I stared at the Bodum and thought about all the other cups of coffee in all the other parts of North America and all of the mornings with all of those men, sitting across from them with my mug, realizing there wasn't much to say, not because the endless human dialogue had run out but because there had been too much intimacy too fast. It was like a drug, another way of losing myself. And, as with all of my addictions, I knew that I shouldn't be doing this even as I couldn't stop myself from doing it.

By the spring of 2001 it was obvious to me that I could not function as I had in previous seasons. I managed to keep up the maintenance side of my business, but I let the other, more lucrative work go. I fell behind in my finances for the first time in my life, and I borrowed money from credit cards with low interest rates. I had never been in debt, and had sworn that I never would be, but I had to admit that I really had no choice. Healing from my trauma and its symptoms was my first priority, because my life was unbearable otherwise.

I was spending yet another afternoon sitting in the chaise longue that I had picked up for ten dollars at a yard sale so many years before. I had hardly been able to eat lately, and it had been days since I'd been outside the house. I could not move my body, but this was nothing new. The debilitation accompanying my depressions was growing, and I could only submit. I was seriously questioning the point of continuing with this journey of rage and pain, but I knew I was too stubborn to end it. Often in the midst of a depression this thought of escape was the only thing that could help me get through.

I felt calm as I sipped my coffee and stared out at the street from the bay window of my living room. Whenever the sun shone, there was a reflection that allowed me to see a faint outline of myself as I stared into the street, into nothingness.

I remained in the chair from about ten in the morning until four in the afternoon. I felt like I had spent the afternoon with Death, and that he and I had talked things through and come to a bargain—but I couldn't remember what it was. I fell into my bed, a queen-sized mattress on the floor, having made the decision that I would no longer live inside this mountain of pain.

Sixteen hours later I woke up. The first thing I thought of was my afternoon with Death. I felt calmer than I had in years—not happy, but indifferent, unequivocal, impassive. I hadn't experienced those feelings for years, perhaps decades, except under the influence of a heavy dose of drugs. I felt that something had snapped inside me, that I had come to the end of something. What that meant, I didn't know or care.

I had swum through oceans of pain, seas of rage, and I was tired, exhausted in a way that no amount of physical labouring could make me. I was pure stillness and I had few thoughts, but one that did enter my consciousness was that I couldn't go on the way that I had been. Something fundamental had to shift. My current life was not worth living, not when I was in a state of constant pain and anxiety.

I got up, made a cup of strong coffee, and went into the living room to sit down in my chair. I felt light, clear, empty. I heard birds singing outside the window again and saw sunlight reach its tendrils up the street and onto my lawn. Hours passed, and eventually I picked up the phone and called Karen. The absolute beauty of having her as a friend was that I could call her up and say anything, and she would understand.

"I spent all day yesterday having a conversation with Death," I told her after we had finished with the preliminaries.

"That must have been interesting," she replied. And in her usual way, Karen drew out everything that had happened to me in the past twenty-four hours. Together we discussed what it might mean. We talked about the long journey we had travelled together, how hard it had been, and how rewarding. I tried to thank her for everything she had done for me, and she told me that it was I who had done it for myself. And then she reminded me of the promise I had made to myself two summers before, when I gave myself a timeline for getting to the bottom of my depressions.

We talked tentatively, because we both knew it was premature; we would be sure of what had happened only as time passed. But that day I had a feeling in my bones that my years of depression were over.

15

WEEPING PILLAR

FROM THAT DAY FORWARD, I woke up every morning feeling calm and peaceful. The constant anxiety I had lived with for decades had receded, and waking up free from depression felt like nothing short of a miracle. I was able to pick up some good contracts to fill in my work schedule, and I went out rock climbing as often as I could.

I had always been intimidated by this medium. It felt less secure than ice and as a result had always brought up a lot more fear for me. Oddly, this is the opposite of how most climbers feel. Meeting Scottie, another climber who was keen to get out a lot, was a big help in overcoming this fear. We became good friends and climbed and trained together as often as we could. Scottie was very methodical about his climbing, and that summer he taught me how to be more strategic as well.

As fall approached, I used the same strategies but tweaked them for my ice climbing. Waterfall ice is rated by a system that goes from grade 2, which is easy low-angle climbing, to grade 6, which is dead vertical. I had always dreamed of climbing grade 6 ice but had not felt confident enough to go out and do it. This became my goal in the winter of 2001/2. In late fall, Scottie and I hiked in to early-season ice climbs, and Karen and I resumed our climbing partnership that winter. Karen knew about my goal and was psyched for me. We decided that the first grade 6 I would hop on would be a climb called Whiteman Falls in Kananaskis Country.

In January 2002 I felt ready. Karen and I left Canmore early in the morning and headed east on the Trans-Canada Highway, then south on Highway 40. We had both climbed Whiteman with other partners, but neither of us had ever led the second pitch, the most difficult section, known to climbers as the crux. After reaching the parking lot, we began the forty-five-minute hike to the base of the climb.

One of the things I always loved about ice climbing was the places it took me. We often skied across lakes and hiked up talus slopes to reach these seasonal sculptures. On this day we hiked up a canyon to reach our objective.

Karen led the first pitch, which was covered in a type of ice called "mushrooms," formed by strong winds. I stared up at the 150-foot pillar whenever I got the chance and mentally broke it down into sections where I would place screws. I knew that I was strong, and that if I needed to I could back off the climb.

When Karen reached the belay and yelled to me that she was secure, I took my belay jacket off and quickly followed the rope over to where she was anchored beneath, and to the left of, the pillar. She gave me encouragement as I racked the ice screws carefully onto my harness. "You are so ready for this," she said. I looked at her and smiled—it was too true. I had been climbing ice for ten years and finally felt I wasn't bringing the weight of the world with me whenever I went into the mountains.

I started up the pitch, and as soon as I left the belay a feeling of complete absorption in the task at hand came over me. Nothing existed but me and the ice, which in this case was as close to vertical as anything I had ever led. I stopped and put in a screw whenever I needed one, then continued on. I felt like a powerhouse, full of energy, and there was never a moment when I doubted my ability to make it to the top of the climb.

About two thirds of the way up the pillar the quality of the ice deteriorated, and it was much more work for me to get good ice axe placements. I put screws in wherever I found a good spot in the unconsolidated ice. Karen could hear the breaking of the chandeliered ice and yelled encouragement to me. When I was past that section, the ice got better and it was a cruise to the top. Once there I put in two screws for my anchor, told Karen I was secure so she could take me off belay, and started pulling in the rope.

I felt on top of the world. I had achieved the goal I had been harbouring for a decade.

The rope came tight and I put it through my belay device and yelled down to Karen that she was on belay. I was happy to see that she found the pitch hard as well.

When she reached the top, her eyes sparkled. "Congratulations, Margo Talbot! That was a beautiful lead." And she gave me a big hug.

I felt overwhelming gratitude for the support she had given me ever since we had met. I had come so far with her encouragement and had attained two of my biggest dreams in life. I vowed to myself that one day I would return Karen's favour.

Soon after this it was time for the fifth annual Canmore Ice Climbing Festival, so Karen and I got busy organizing the event with Mike. It had become an annual routine for us, and we found the workload easier with each passing year. Although we loved every aspect of the event, the highlight was the Saturday night party at Hooligans Pub, where we could relax from our duties and gear up for a night of dancing.

We arrived at Hooligans early, and I was surprised to see fellow climber Sean Elliott at the bar. I had known Sean when I lived in Jasper all those years ago, and although I had run into him from time to time, it was a rare event. He introduced me to his friend Dave, and we saw each other off and on throughout the evening. During one of my breaks from dancing, I went over to talk with them. They told me about their plans to do some climbing around Jasper near the end of March and invited me to come along. I got the dates, as well as Dave's phone number, and the plan was laid.

Ice-climbing season was almost over when I headed to Jasper, but I was still feeling strong and was keen to climb the classics I had dreamed about when I first started in the sport. When they invited me along, Sean and Dave had told me they would give me every crux lead on the trip. At the time I thought this was just a joke, but it turned out they did precisely that. We started with Aussi Beau Que C'en a L'aire, a beautiful ribbon of ice on Mount Klapperhorn, which is just across the highway from Mount Robson. This was steep and featured, and really fun to climb. The following day we went to Curtain Call, a climb that had always intimidated me, not only because of its difficulty but also because of the fracture across the sheet of ice that comprises the last, and often crux, pitch. I had never broken a pick while ice climbing before, but I broke two while leading the curtain. I chalked this up to the cold, as it was minus thirty degrees when we were gearing up at the base.

We saved the best for last. On our third day we drove down the Icefields Parkway to Weeping Pillar. Sean had been on the climb the week before and warned me about the final and crux pitch. "It was scary, all chandeliered, and it was unconsolidated in places. I hated it, but you'll like it." If he was trying to reassure me, he wasn't doing a good job of it.

"I'll go up and have a look," I replied. "If I don't like it, I'll back off."

We cruised up the bottom four pitches, lining up our leads so that I would get the seventh and final pitch. When we finally reached the base of it, I saw what Sean had been talking about.

"You're right," I said, "it looks sketchy. I'll head up, and if it doesn't feel right I'll come back down." I carefully racked my equipment, and Dave put me on belay.

The beauty is to approach a climb and know very little about what you will encounter. You carry skills and experience from which to draw the card that fits the hand. You compare a pitch to one you've climbed before; you see a challenge through the eyes of a past success. Years of experience were with me now. I felt intimidated, but that feeling faded as soon as I started to climb. I became so engaged with the process that nothing else mattered. I felt at peace.

The pitch turned out to be hard grade 6, by far the most challenging I'd ever led. But I felt confident in my abilities. The ice quality was bad and the protection sketchy: it was the kind of pitch I swore I would never lead when I started ice climbing. But I had been different then, the girl who thought every decision she made brought her closer to disaster. Now I was moving within a new form, still me and yet more me, with a trust of self I had never known. I stayed present and didn't enter into the dance of fear that had once ruled my life.

I brought Sean and Dave up to the belay, and they both congratulated me on my lead. We shared a snack and some hot chocolate while we set up for the rappels. We got back to the truck just after dark and drove to the Astoria Bar, where we celebrated our climb with standard fare: French fries, hamburgers, and dark beer.

It had now been nine months since I had come out of my last great depression, and my confidence on ice got me fired up for another rock-climbing season. Through the spring of 2002, when the weather in the Rockies is usually wet and cold, I stayed strong by running and training in the gym. As soon as it was warm enough, I drove up to a local crag and traversed back and forth on the featured rock. A friend had introduced me to techno music, and I blasted this through my headphones as I moved horizontally across the rock. When the weather warmed up more, I got in touch with some of my climbing partners and went out on some real routes.

In the middle of August, I had just come home from a day at Grassi Lakes and was really psyched. I had successfully climbed a route that I had always fallen on, and I was preparing a favourite meal, seafood fettuccine, in the kitchen. As I poured myself a glass of red wine, the phone rang. I assumed it was one of my friends inviting me to a party, or perhaps a client calling to find out when I could begin work on their landscape. But it was Tony, Jay's foreman on the construction site in Whistler.

When I heard his voice on the line I felt a mixture of emotions. Tony and I had not spoken for over ten years, so I knew a call from him could mean only one thing.

"Jay died two days ago," he said after we'd exchanged greetings. "Complications with his liver. I knew you would want to know."

I did want to know, but the news sent my heart reeling. Jay and I had had an abrupt split, and I had always wondered if we would ever run into each other again and talk about what had happened all those years ago. Now I realized I would never have that sort of closure. Whatever conclusions I had come up with on my own in the past thirteen years would have to suffice.

Tony and I chatted for a few more minutes before ending the call. I didn't feel like eating anymore, so I drew a hot bath, lit a candle, and climbed into the tub with my glass of wine.

Jay may have been an addict and a criminal, but he had been a life-altering agent of change for me. Through him I had gained knowledge of a world that most people only know through books or movies. And I had been able to experience pure, unadulterated love for the only time in my life. After my time with Jay, I no longer took anything in the world at face value, least of all what is commonly referred to as romantic love.

After soaking for what felt like hours, I dried myself off and fell into the oblivion of sleep.

16

BLUE ANGEL

Every year the Banff Mountain Film Festival acknowledges a person who has made a significant contribution to mountain life in the Canadian Rockies and presents him or her with the Summit of Excellence Award. In November 2002, that award went to Barry Blanchard. I usually skipped the party that accompanied the award, but this year I couldn't wait to honour Barry for his achievements. The party, held in Canmore on the opening night of the festival that year, was also a great chance to see many people from the climbing world in one place.

Karen and I arranged to meet at her place on November 1, the night of the party. As I entered the house she and Brad now lived in, she called from the bathroom: "Let me see your pants!"

I had told her about the orange faux-vinyl pants I had bought for the occasion. Karen and I had a long history of competing with each other in the areas of outrageous clothing, sparkle jewellery, and glitter makeup. The ante rose every time we attempted to outdo each other, and Karen's outfit for the evening was far from diffident: a zebra-print skirt with red tassels around the hem, black pumps and a tight black shirt.

Kim Csizmazia arrived shortly after I did. She had recently moved to town, and Karen and I quickly decided that she was a lot of fun. Kim and I had brought bottles of red wine, so we uncorked one and sat down to catch up with each other's news. We drank and laughed and complimented each other on our wardrobes until we couldn't stand it anymore.

"Let's go!" I said. "It's eight-thirty and I don't want to miss one minute of the party." I had been too busy primping to have consumed much wine. "Hop in my truck. I'll drive."

After arriving at the party, I made my way through the main room, stopping briefly to chat with friends, while Karen covered everyone's cheeks with blue glitter. Whenever the two of us went out to a significant social affair, she brought along tubes of lip gloss and a jar of glitter and would not rest until she had convinced everyone in the room to brighten up their faces. It was crowded, and Karen mentioned there was a room at the back that was quieter, where we could escape the noise and congestion.

I followed her into the room, where she promptly sat down in what I thought was the last chair. Then I spied an empty wheelchair in the middle of the room. I sat down in it and was amazed at how comfortable and light it was. After forty-five minutes of wheeling around, socializing, it occurred to me that somebody might actually need to use the chair. I scanned the room, and it didn't take me long to find the owner: there was a man with no legs sitting on a bench near the wall.

I wheeled over to him and asked if he needed his chair.

"Oh no, you go ahead and use it," he replied. "But thanks for asking."

I noticed he had blue sparkles all over his face. "I see Karen's been here with her jar of glitter," I said.

We started chatting, and it turned out that Warren was in Canmore to present a film he had entered in the festival.

I didn't move from the room for the rest of the evening, except to get Warren and myself more drinks. Toward the end of the evening he pulled a book out from under his chair and handed it to me. *A Test of Will* was a book he had written about his accident. He told me the screening times for his film and invited me to come and watch it on one of the days it was being featured.

On Sunday I made the twenty-minute drive from Canmore to Banff, timing it so that I arrived a few hours early so I could do some visiting with friends before Warren's film screened. I was not disappointed; after living in the Rocky Mountains for eighteen years, and attending the festival for more than ten, I knew a fair number of people. Just as I was wondering if there were still tickets available for the show, Kim walked up to me and handed me hers. "I'm leaving. Here's my ticket, if you want it."

I took my seat in the theatre, and within minutes the film was introduced and began to roll. *The Second Step* chronicled Warren's trip to the remote Federation Peak in Tasmania. It showed a flashback of him trapped under a one-ton rock and the subsequent loss of both his legs, and then described how he decided he wanted to get back into the wilderness, and how this climb was the culmination of twenty months of training. All I could think as I watched the film was, *This guy's got to try ice climbing.*

I had just finished helping my ex-husband, Joe, put together the latest edition of *Waterfall Ice Climbs in the Canadian Rockies* and had a few copies of it with me in my pack. When I got out of the theatre, I looked for Warren. He was on his way to an interview in the media room, but he had a few minutes to chat. I handed him the guide, saying, "Here's a copy of the local ice-climbing guidebook. If you ever decide you want to try ice climbing, send me an email." He thanked me and invited me to go to the media room with him and out to dinner after the interview.

I accepted Warren's dinner invitation and was astounded at how much attention was focused on him as he cruised around the restaurant in his wheelchair. He was different from most men I had met, more open, less driven by his ego, and I wondered if that had anything to do with his accident. He was also clearly a deep thinker.

As we were finishing our meal, he asked if I thought we should go back to the film festival for the awards ceremony.

"The only reason to go back," I replied, "would be if you thought your film was going to win."

Warren laughed, and we ordered another round of drinks.

When we were finally ready to leave, there was still time to catch the end of the awards ceremony. We entered through the VIP doors using Warren's pass and sat down. The place was packed; I couldn't believe there were so many people with the patience to sit through hours of accolades and acceptance speeches.

We had arrived just as the Grand Prize-winning film was to be announced, and Warren's jaw dropped when "*The Second Step*!" boomed over the sound system. He jumped into his wheelchair to go up on stage and receive the award. Afterward he disappeared backstage, where his accomplishment was being celebrated. I knew he would be taking a taxi to the airport within hours, so I said goodbye and went home to bed.

Warren soon returned to Australia to prepare for an upcoming expedition to Mount Kilimanjaro, but a week later he sent me an email, telling me he would be in North America in one month for a meeting and that he could stop over and do some ice climbing with me if I was still interested in taking him out. I replied that if he gave me the dates, I would pick him up at the Calgary airport and we would get out on the ice for a few days.

Now that the reality of the situation was upon me, I was overwhelmed. Where should I take him, and how would I climb with a legless guy? I decided that it might be a good idea to have another person with us, an ice climber who was skilled enough to help me troubleshoot whatever scenario arose. I immediately thought of Kim's partner, Will Gadd, a professional athlete who had taken many sports, including ice climbing, to their highest level. I had always admired his keen mind and his aptitude for problem solving, and I knew that between the two of us we could figure this thing out. Will is a people person, and I suspected he would like the challenge. My one concern was that he was also a really busy person and perhaps didn't need another item on his plate. But I called him anyway.

"I'm in. It sounds like fun," he said when I told him about the plan.

One month later we were on our way into Marble Canyon. Warren hiked in on his prosthetic legs and arm crutches, with his crampon attachments in his pack. Everything went smoothly. Will rigged up a system to lower two climbers at a time into the canyon, and we took turns getting lowered onto the ice next to Warren, who was a natural: he had tremendous upper-body strength and an incredibly tenacious mind. Satisfied that we had it figured out, Warren and I went to Weeping Wall the next day and did laps on the first pitch. That was when he told me about a plan that he and a friend had cooked up.

The previous winter, while he was in Telluride, Colorado, Warren had met Michael O'Donnell, a climber I had known for ten years. Michael had been climbing with Erik Weihenmayer, and their partnership had culminated in Erik's being the first blind person to summit Mount Everest. Michael was adamant that if Erik could climb ice, so could Warren, and he said that once Warren had trained sufficiently, they would climb the Central Pillar of Weeping Wall. I was keen to be involved, and after we talked to Michael, the three of us decided we would plan the climb as soon as Warren returned from his trip to Mount Kilimanjaro in March 2003.

When Will found out what we were doing, he insisted that something this cool had to be filmed, so he cleared his schedule and came along with his video camera; Kim, who would do all the rigging; and Brad Wrobleski, who agreed to film the long shots.

The climb, when it happened, went more smoothly than any of us could have imagined. Everyone was focused on getting Warren to the top of Weeping Wall, and eight hours after leaving the parking lot we were at the top of one of the world's most renowned ice climbs. Michael and I had no idea how tricky it would be to get Warren off the climb. We had just assumed that he would rappel, but with no articulation in his prosthetic legs he couldn't really lower himself down this way. Finally we devised a system by which Michael lowered us both at once. In this way we made it back down to the ground and our vehicles before dark.

Before Warren had returned to Canada to climb Weeping Wall, we had decided that he would stay in Canmore after we made the film and that we would move in together. It was a bold move for both of us, and it brought up a lot of my old fears—I had never had a healthy, or long-term, relationship—but since we would otherwise be living on opposite sides of the planet, we felt it was our best option to explore the deep connection that had blossomed between us and see where it might take us. Meshing our two lives would turn out to be an interesting journey for both of us.

In the meantime, I started another season of landscaping while Warren got busy establishing himself as a speaker in North America. As usual during the summer months, I dreamed of the crisp, cold days of autumn and the thought of ice forming high in the alpine. And for the first time I dreamed of travelling. I had received an email from Erin Eddy, representing the Ouray Ice Festival in southwestern Colorado, who was looking for women climbers to compete at the 2004 event. During all my years of climbing I had watched my friends and fellow climbers go down to compete in the event, but I was never sure I could handle the stress of competing or travelling. In 1997 I had competed in the ice-climbing events at the ESPN X-Games at Big Bear Lake, California, but was ill-prepared for the accompanying stress. I had always imagined the day when I would no longer be too depressed to travel or to train for a competition, and now I filled out the Ouray application form and sent it in.

Within a month I received a letter from Erin telling me that I had been selected to compete in the women's division at the upcoming festival. I told myself that I would do everything in my power to be climbing as well as I could by the time the event rolled around. I went to Canmore's indoor climbing gym and got my hands and arms as strong as possible, and I went out mixed climbing at every opportunity. This sport, in which participants climb on rock using ice axes and crampons—usually, but not always, to gain access to isolated pieces of ice—had become popular in recent years.

In early January 2004, Warren and I drove down to Ouray, a picturesque town in the San Juan Mountains. When we got there we found ourselves among many people I knew from my years of climbing, including quite a few from Canmore. The event was slated to start on Friday night, with the competition on Saturday and climbing clinics on Sunday. I went home early Friday evening to get well rested, but I couldn't relax and barely slept. I knew myself well enough to expect this, and I knew many other competitors would also be sleepless that night.

We had drawn straws at the athletes' meeting, and I was going to be the second climber on the route in the morning. I was in the canyon at 8 a.m. and did warm-up exercises while the first climber went up the route. There weren't many spectators out this early, which was a relief. When it was my turn I walked up to the ice, so nervous I could barely think. The route started with a section of ice and then moved onto a rock traverse that trended left. All of the protection on the climb had been preplaced: ice screws for the bottom section and bolts along the rock traverse.

I was a far better ice climber than mixed climber, and I cruised up the bottom portion of the route. At the top I clipped the rope into the pre-placed bolt and headed left onto the traverse. I could hear people cheering from the viewing platform above, and at one point I heard Karen yell, "Nice work, Bitch!" This was her term of endearment for me, and I smiled as I heard her familiar voice from above. But my mind went blank as I headed out onto the rock traverse: far from being focused, I was a bag of nerves.

Soon after I clipped the third bolt, I came off, and as I fell through the air my ice axe flew from my left hand and fell to the bottom of the canyon. The belayers lowered me to the ground while the crowd cheered me for my attempt on the route. I was happy that the stressful part of the festival was over, and I walked out of the canyon and up to the bridge, where I knew I would find Karen.

Saturday night was the social highlight of the festival, and as is usual at such events there was partying and dancing. This year the organizers had asked for athletes to volunteer to model themselves on a makeshift runway while members of the audience bid for their services. The winning bidder got to go climbing with the featured athlete the following day, and the ice park put the money toward its operating costs.

Luckily I was travelling with a pair of sparkly red pants that Karen had given me just months before. I complemented these with my cowboy boots and a white tank top studded with red stars. The audience loved my pants from the moment I stepped onto the catwalk. When the MC opened up the bidding, one man in particular seemed hell-bent on climbing with me. He was tall, blond, and very fit. We were briefly introduced when the auction ended, and we made arrangements to meet the following morning.

Dan Nordstrom owns the Seattle-based sports-apparel company Outdoor Research. Although he is very athletic, he had not done much ice climbing. He had a few technical weaknesses, which he quickly corrected during the day. After some initial instruction we took turns doing laps, and we had a great day talking and climbing in the canyon.

On our way out of the park, I asked Dan if he wanted to meet Warren. We didn't need to go far to find him, since he was standing on the lower bridge as we left the canyon. The three of us chatted for a while, and as were about to part company Dan asked, "Would you two be interested in representing my company as sponsored athletes?" We replied that we would be honoured to do so, and the three of us made plans to meet later that evening for dinner. I was elated; other than Karen's enthusiastic care, I had never had much outside support, and Dan's offer felt like a huge validation. After spending the day with him, I felt that working with his company would be relaxed and fun.

We met for dinner that night at a Mexican restaurant. As we sipped our first round of margaritas, Dan told us that he had bought the company seven months earlier, after its owner and founder, Ron Gregg, had died in an avalanche in British Columbia. In addition to making some of the best climbing accessories on the market, Outdoor Research had recently acquired a women's clothing line and was in its first year of making apparel for men. I had previous experience testing clothing for other companies, but the prospect of being involved with a line that was new to the market excited both Warren and me.

My fortieth birthday was fast approaching. I had always told myself that I would change my life at forty, but I had no idea what that change would look like. Within a month of returning from Ouray, Warren and I decided to move to Vancouver so that we could both make a shift in our careers. We timed the move for the spring. It was a huge step for me. Other than my brief stint with Jay, I had never spent much time in a city, and I had never been part of a community or a network of friends anywhere but in Canmore. I had made the mountains and the sports I pursued in them the focus of my life since arriving there twenty years before, but now I wanted an opportunity to see what else I could do with my talents.

Because it had never really been celebrated when I was growing up, I made a point of hosting my own birthday party every year. I was working in Canmore's second-hand gear store, Switching Gear, that winter, when Mark Cosslett, a man I was acquainted with but didn't know that well, walked in and struck up a conversation with me. The topic of my approaching birthday somehow came up, and Mark said, "Let's celebrate it at my place. It's time I threw a big party!"

I was surprised, but in the following weeks he and I organized a big party to be held at his condo in one of the newer developments in town. All my friends were there, and it felt like a going-away party in addition to a celebration of my birthday. I drank gin and tonics all night while I socialized with my friends. In the middle of it all, Will walked over and handed me a gift—a ten-centimetre Black Diamond ice screw. He had written a note on the cardboard packaging: *For the Good Times to Come.* As I read the message, I was struck by the realization that my depression-free years had just begun, and that turning forty was the beginning of the best part of my life.

Five days later, Warren and I packed up and moved to Vancouver. The fact that I was moving back to the city where I had spent so much time when I was involved with Jay did not escape my notice, but I had come so far and grown so much that it felt like another lifetime. Vancouver is a big city, and none of Jay's contacts had lived there anyway, so I felt the connection was too vague to have any direct impact on me. Warren and I rented a 650-square-foot condo on the twenty-sixth floor of a high-rise in Yaletown, and began our new adventure.

In those days Vancouver had a booming film industry that employed thousands of people; it was known for providing interesting work and good pay. My sister Jane, who was living there and working in film, encouraged me to apply to one of the local unions as soon as I arrived. I did so, but found the job taxing, in part because it was the first time I had worked indoors since I was employed at the Village Mart at sixteen. I felt like a part of me was dying, living in a city where I had so little connection to nature. Then I had an interesting idea.

While I was at Switching Gear in Canmore, I had met a woman named Denise who had worked as a guide in Antarctica. I questioned her extensively about her experiences there and became captivated by the idea of visiting this remote continent. She had given me the contact details for Mike Sharpe, the man who did the hiring for the company, and told me I could use her as a reference. I hadn't thought about it much further, but within a few months of moving to Vancouver I sent Mike an email— and heard back from him straight away. We exchanged emails for about a month. Then he told me I would be receiving a contract in the mail for the upcoming season on the ice, which would run from November 2004 to January 2005. I was ecstatic: when it comes to wilderness, there are few places wilder than Antarctica. In less than six months I'd be heading off on the adventure of a lifetime.

17

POLAR CIRCUS

ANTARCTIC LOGISTICS AND EXPEDITIONS is the biggest and most impressive guiding operation working in the interior of the southern continent. When he forwarded my contract from ALE's Salt Lake City offices, Operations Manager Mike Sharpe also sent me some reading material so I could get up to speed on what to expect in terms of weather, flights, work duties, and the gear that I would need for my season down there.

As well as hiring guides for its guests, ALE coordinated all the logistics of getting people in and out of the interior of Antarctica. Clients flew in every ten to fourteen days and stayed from two weeks to two months. Some people came to do the full ski trip from the edge of the continent to the geographic South Pole, which takes approximately two months, whereas others wanted to ski in from the last degree of latitude, a twelve- to fourteen-day adventure. Many guests were in Antarctica to climb Mount Vinson, one of the Seven Summits—the highest peaks on each of the seven continents. Mount Vinson is positioned in the middle of the Ellsworth Mountains. Our base camp at Patriot Hills was on the southern end of this mountain chain. Personal living space for all trips took the form of small nylon tents; larger structures called Weatherhavens were used for dining and socializing. These specialized tents were designed to withstand extreme weather conditions, particularly heavy winds.

The staging ground for ALE's trips was Punta Arenas, a city at the southernmost tip of Chile, where ALE has a local office. Here we boarded an Ilyushin 76 jet and flew four and a half hours to the interior of Antarctica.

The first time I landed in Antarctica, I could hardly believe where I was. The jet had just landed on a three-mile runway of ice, scoured clear by the katabatic winds that come rolling down from the interior of the Polar Plateau, five hundred miles away. Everything looked and felt out of the ordinary, including the interior of the aircraft. There were fifty-five passengers on the plane, staff as well as clients, all sitting on small seats that folded down from each side of the aircraft. Seventeen tons of cargo, mainly gear and fresh food, filled the centre of the plane between the seats. The cargo also included the equipment needed for ongoing operations at the main camp.

When the season's first crew arrived, they would find only a bamboo stake in the ground. This marked the entrance to an underground labyrinth of ice tunnels and caves that had been burrowed out over the years. Everything needed to set up camp was stored under the ice. The first crew had the task of digging up the tents and setting up camp in the extreme weather of an Antarctic spring. Only when a rudimentary camp was set up would the rest of the crew be flown in.

Antarctica is a desert, receiving less than two inches of precipitation a year. If I were to describe the place in one word, I would say "windy." While living down there, I experienced winds blowing at over one hundred miles per hour. This is the kind of wind that can pick up fist-sized chunks of ice and pelt you in the face with them. You don't really want to go out in that kind of weather, but you have no choice if you need to tighten the tie-downs on your tent or go to the washroom. In Antarctica, you have no doubt that nature is in control.

On the other hand, great wilderness offers a space that is free from the trappings of mankind and modern society. I had taken our psychically busy culture as a given, but after a few weeks in "the desolate continent" I began to notice the absence of an assault on my senses. No billboards, no traffic, no Starbucks on every corner—life was boiled down to its most basic necessities.

The most interesting part of living in Antarctica was observing what happened to me when I had to deal with the absence of external stimuli for a prolonged period. My mental chatter began to subside, replaced by feelings, thoughts, and desires that welled up from inside me. I had no idea how long these feelings had been dampened, but I realized that I had not been able to hear myself think while living amidst the noise and confusion of North American culture. Now, in the absence of the cacophony and in the presence of nature's peace, I was able to feel new things.

I also began to ask myself, "If I am not aware of my deepest truths, then whose truths am I living by?" The deeper I dove into this, the more I realized how much my consciousness had been hijacked by outside influences. I began to feel grateful for my depressions; they had led me more deeply into myself than any period of normalcy or mania had. I also began to value my years of therapy, for they had taught me how to deal with my emotions by tracking them very closely. Everything became a blessing that had led me to this realization: the only thing that mattered was that I follow the direction of my own heart in this world.

Paradoxically, I found that the hardest part of living and working in Antarctica was the lack of contact with the rest of the world. We had only limited email access and could purchase satellite phone cards that cost a dollar a minute. I had always been comfortable spending a lot of time alone, and I liked to be self-sufficient, but I had a distinct feeling of being cut off from the world while living there. During the first season, I was so caught up in the novelty of it all that I dealt with the isolation pretty well. The independence that characterized my relationship with Warren actually benefited me while working on the ice. We were living quite autonomous lives despite being together as a couple, and this made it easier for me to accept limited contact with him for the three months that I was living in Antarctica. It also made it easier for me not to lose my space to him as I had done in my previous relationships. This new-found ability to maintain healthy boundaries within an intimate relationship, combined with the underlying stability of our emotional bond, allowed me to move forward in my life in ways that I had never previously had the focus to do.

When the first season ended, I was completely unprepared for the shock I felt upon my return to civilization. When we flew in to Punta Arenas, I was struck by the conveniences there. Things I had taken for granted all my life had become great luxuries. Riding in the shuttle from the airport to our hotel was a treat after months of moving around on skis or by snowmobile in minus-thirty temperatures. Once in my hotel room, I didn't want to give up the proximity to my own bathroom and a bed with actual sheets and blankets. Running water felt like a dream, and the fact it came out hot as well as cold seemed a miracle. I immediately took a hot bath—my first real cleansing in over two months. Eventually I got hungry and left the hotel room. Outside I was greeted by the sight of traffic, which was now a novelty to me. I marvelled at the stores, where I could enter and buy whatever I wanted or needed—food, toiletries, a hot coffee. There were trees and flowers and the exotic smells that accompanied them. It was a symphony for my senses, and I revelled in every aspect of it.

The following afternoon I was driven back to the airport to catch an overnight flight to Houston. One quick connection got me on a non-stop flight into Vancouver, where Warren was waiting to pick me up at the airport. Twenty minutes later, back in our apartment, I still marvelled at the presence of running water, electricity, and central heating. I found it hard to believe that I could walk two blocks in any direction and get a latte, a bottle of wine, or sushi, or that I could fill my tank with gas and drive anywhere, anytime, and refill it when it ran low. Although the culture shock wore off after a few months, my appreciation of these things did not.

Seeing Warren for the first time after being gone for ten weeks, I realized that it was time for us to put more focus on, and to make some decisions about, our relationship. I no longer wanted to live in a glass tower, where I kept a wall up around me so I could feel safe. Before I left for Antarctica, we had discussed the distance between us and decided that we were both ready to take our relationship to a deeper level. Given my trust issues and my fear of getting close to anybody, we agreed we needed help to move through this. But we had no idea where to turn. I called Jane, who had always been my best resource in my healing journey. She recommended a meditation school where she and her partner, Stepan, had taken some courses and experienced great benefit. I filed the advice in the back of my mind, intending to revisit it when I returned from Antarctica. But over dinner that evening, Warren told me that he had signed up for the meditation courses while I was gone.

"You've got to sign up," he enthused. "They're amazing. I didn't know I would actually like doing this kind of inner work. You're going to love it."

. I made an appointment with the school's founder and signed up for level one meditation. When I completed it, Warren and I signed up for level two and ended up going through four levels over two years. Our meditation journey was filled with wonderful surprises as we realized that the issues surfacing in our relationship had been present in every earlier relationship we'd had, as well as in all other aspects of our lives. Meditation allowed us to focus on our core issues instead of their myriad manifestations. And I began to glimpse the inner peace I had been trying to experience throughout my life. It was the perfect next step after my decades of talk therapy.

The atmosphere at the school was accepting and supportive, a welcome respite from what I had come to expect from most of the world. Each student spent time examining their wounds, then cleared and healed them in order to move on in life. The instructor showed us how to let go of patterns that no longer served us, and taught us how to replace these defunct patterns with new belief structures that validated and supported where we wanted to go as well as who we wanted to be. Classes were held only twice each week, but part of the deal was that we would meditate every day on our own—first for half an hour, and then for an hour. The benefits I received from these courses were many, and they took my healing to a new level.

Two weeks after I returned to Vancouver, Warren called me with some great news: "I just got an offer to do a talk on a cruise ship in Antarctica—and you're invited to come along with me!"

A month later we flew to Ushuaia, a city at the southern tip of Argentina, where we boarded the Peregrine Adventures cruise ship. Peregrine, a company started by Andrew Prossin out of Vancouver, followed the highest standards for polar cruises, paying great attention to the guest experience, and also adhering to some of the most environmentally conscious codes in the tourism industry. Warren and I were awed by the beauty of the Antarctic Peninsula, and we vowed that it would not be our last trip to that part of the world.

At the end of the cruise, Andrew asked if we would like to be part of the expedition crew for their upcoming season in the High Arctic. We quickly accepted the offer, and in July 2005, Warren and I flew to Norway to work with Peregrine out of Svalbard. For me, this was another dream job. We lived like guests on board a Russian ice-strengthened ship, ate fabulous meals, and visited historical sights. Our job was to take the guests on hikes and Zodiac rides, to give them lots of information about the region they were visiting, and to give presentations on board the ship when we were at sea. Warren and I did two trips out of Svalbard before returning to Vancouver in August.

In November I was on my way back down to South America, my love affair with the Canadian Rockies having been extended to encompass remote wilderness everywhere. We were scheduled to fly to Antarctica a few days after I arrived in Punta Arenas, but the weather at the main camp of Patriot Hills was too unsettled for us to even consider trying to get in. Ninety-knot winds had been blowing as the camp staff tried to get a minimal shelter set up for our arrival. We waited in the small coastal town without complaint. We were still being paid and just enjoyed the food and accommodation provided by ALE.

Twelve days later we flew down onto the ice. Although we were grateful for the work the initial crew had already done, there was still a lot more to do. Our headquarters was a smaller Weatherhaven, around which we set up our cozy personal tents—two-person nylon tents, with an optional twin mattress inside and all of our personal gear. (I got a good sense of how little I needed while I was living in Antarctica.) We still needed to set up the main dining tent, the largest tent of all, as well as the smallest of the Weatherhavens to serve as our toilets. Events progressed like molasses in winter, as the cold and wind prevented us from staying out in the elements for more than two hours at a time. Thankfully there were many of us, because it took all our hands working in concert to build the camp. It seemed to take forever, but we were finally putting in the last details: the water maker, the propane stove, the counters, the plastic tables and chairs. It was pretty bare bones, but it felt luxurious compared with what we had when we first landed.

Four days after I arrived, I was flown into Vinson Base Camp. We were now two weeks behind schedule and needed to get up there to dig out the guides' tent, set up our personal tents, and put up the radio line as well as the solar panels that we relied on for power in all our camps.

Finally the first wave of clients flew in. Heather and Neill, my fellow guides, went up the mountain with clients while I stayed behind to manage

Base Camp. Three days into their scheduled five-day ascent, in the middle of the afternoon, I was lying in my tent inside a sleeping bag, wearing a down parka and pants. I had not experienced such cold temperatures at Vinson the previous year, and I had never heard anyone speak of such extremes during the summer months. Everything was in danger of freezing: the medical supplies, the eggs, and—God forbid—the beer and wine. At first I brought all these necessities into my tent in the hope that they would get more solar radiation here than in the Weatherhaven that served as the main shelter. But even here, where the temperature was usually a lot warmer, my pocket thermometer was registering minus-thirty degrees without the wind chill factor.

The winds were another thing. For two nights in a row I thought my tent would take flight. The windward side was being blown in with such force that the poles were often flattened against my body, and I could feel the vibration of the mattress as the wind crept under the floor of my tent.

When I eventually got back to Patriot Hills, the camp manager asked if I had been scared while waiting out that storm.

"Not for an instant," I replied. "If nature wants to take me down, I'll go willingly. But if another human being wants to mess with me, I'll fight to the bitter end."

Not long after I returned from Vinson Base Camp, I had two clients arrive for a Last Degree trip to the South Pole. In this excursion, skiers are dropped off at 89° south latitude and then ski the sixty nautical miles (sixty-nine statute miles) to the geographic South Pole. I had managed to get everything ready for the trip before they arrived, despite the early-season delay. We spent a couple of days making sure their ski setups worked, and I had them practise setting up their tent in high winds. Then we got the weather we needed for the long flight south to the 89th parallel.

These two turned out to be among the best clients I have ever had—which, to a guide, means that she feels like she is out with buddies but is actually getting paid to go where she wants to go. My clients and I skied and hauled all our equipment in pulks, specialized sleds designed for the polar environment. Each day we got up at 8 a.m., ate breakfast, and then set off, with our gear and tents packed, at 10 a.m. sharp. I would head out first, breaking trail and navigating in the 360-degree whiteness that was our landscape. We would typically ski until 6 p.m., after covering as many miles as we could. We then set up our tents, dug a toilet pit sheltered from the wind, and hunkered down for a night of eating, drinking tea, and resting our tired bodies.

On day three I was feeling particularly tired. It had been a long season, and I still had one last mountain trip to do before it ended. I was tired not only from the day's work but also from the temperatures, which were much colder than they had been the previous year, and from the whiteout conditions we were travelling in. It took a lot of extra energy to navigate toward our destination when I could see only fifty feet in front of us as we skied. Under clear skies, polar travellers take a GPS reading every hour, then line their direction up with their shadow, a cloud formation, or the angle of the Sastrugi (the wave-like formations on the ground formed by high winds). But in whiteout conditions none of these factors can be relied on, so readings are taken more frequently with a compass or GPS.

After we set up camp, my two clients got into their tent, and I into mine. I could tell they were as tired as I was from battling the elements. I changed into my sleeping thermals, put on my down pants and parka, and crawled into my sleeping bag with my water bottle, which I had filled with hot water made from melted snow. The stove hissed beside me, and I found the sound soothing: it created the white noise I needed to feel some privacy, some sort of barrier between myself and my clients. I enjoyed spending my days with them, but I also needed my personal downtime each evening.

While the next pot of snow was turning into boiling water for my tea, I got out my journal, something I take everywhere I go, including the South Pole. I have been putting my thoughts on paper ever since that day in English class when I was fifteen and discovered writing as an outlet. On this evening I was feeling strangely sad, and exquisitely alone, even though there were two other people not fifteen feet from my tent. This was not simply the loneliness of a woman who had been in a remote wilderness for two months, but rather the aloneness of a lifetime of feeling misunderstood, separate, and completely outside of any tribe. The loneliness I felt was more acute than it had ever been, and I lay back and allowed myself to bathe in its intensity.

The sound of the water boiling pulled me out of this state. In order not to waste fuel I had to either pour the water into my thermos or add more snow to be melted. I made my thermos of peppermint tea, leaving just enough liquid in the bottom of the pot to start the process all over again and boil the water that would rehydrate my dinner.

I returned to my journal and the attempt to craft my feelings into words. As I wrote I was hit with the realization that relationships are the most important thing in our lives—more important than anything else we accomplish or do. In the end we are nothing but the sum total of how we have affected others in this world, for better or for worse. This was a startling revelation to me. I had spent my life keeping myself safe from people and proving how strong I was, how little I needed anybody. I started to make a list of the people who had meant the most to me in my life, and I vowed to re-establish, as well as strengthen, my connection with them as soon as I got off this ice-capped continent.

I also realized that the strongest and longest-lasting relationship I'd had in my life was with the living landscape. Nature had been my healer and my teacher. I had returned to nature again and again when I could no longer cope within the human-made confines of civilization.

I wondered what the future held for the planet, and what I might do to be part of its healing. I knew that wilderness was disappearing at an alarming rate, and that at some point there would be so little left that most humans would never have a chance to see untamed nature. I asked myself what this meant for future generations, who might never know the deep connection I experienced daily. But I mostly wondered what a little Margo of the future would do; where would she go to get away from this destructive culture and find peace and rejuvenation? What did the future hold for humanity if this was lost and there was no place left in which to find this deep connection with the universe?

The second pot of water had reached a boil, so I opened the foil pouch that contained my dehydrated dinner, poured the water in, and resealed the pouch for the required five minutes before opening it again. Focusing on dinner helped me emerge from my reverie, and by the time I finished eating, my thoughts had returned to my immediate goal: getting my clients to the South Pole.

After my trip to the Pole, I had one last job to do before my season ended: taking a client to the top of Mount Vinson. Rob was in Antarctica to climb the sixth peak in his bid to do the Seven Summits. He was in decent shape, and had an iron will that I knew would serve him well on our ascent. As we flew to Vinson, he was captivated by the scenery throughout the Ellsworth Mountains, and upon landing at Base Camp we had a view for hundreds of miles toward the Polar Plateau and the South Pole itself. The camp sat below the west face of Mount Vinson, its serac-covered flanks interspersed with smoother, more homogeneous, ridgelines and gullies.

Heather and Neill, who had been guiding the mountain all season, were there to greet us, and that evening we held a meeting in the guides' tent. It was late in the season; we were the last group going up the mountain and would be alone on its flanks. Heather would accompany Rob and me up the mountain, while Neill would stay behind to handle radio calls and begin breaking down Base Camp.

We spent our first day in camp acclimatizing. We ate, rehydrated, and went over crevasse rescue techniques with Rob. We discussed the schedule for climbing the mountain and laid out the timeline we would be following. I had checked Rob's gear before leaving Patriot Hills, but now I made him go over it again, just to be sure.

As the highest point on the Antarctic continent, Vinson is on the hit list of many mountaineers. It is technically a massif, a compact group of connected mountains forming an independent portion of a range. There are many routes up the 16,050-foot peak, some more difficult and direct than others. The most commonly climbed route meanders up the Branscomb Glacier and around buttresses, giving the climber one of the longest but least difficult passages to the top. Most parties take a day to acclimatize at Base Camp, then spend an easy day travelling with a light pack and a small sled up to Low Camp, which is situated at nine thousand feet. Once you leave Low Camp, you must carry everything on your back up steeper terrain to the site of High Camp, situated on Vinson's summit plateau.

The biggest danger to visitors in the harsh Antarctic landscape is the threat of hypothermia or frostbite. Ambient air temperatures get colder the higher the altitude, and there is always the wind chill to take into account. As guides, we had to be vigilant to ensure that our clients—who had each paid around $35,000 to attempt the mountain—didn't leave some part of their skin exposed.

Heather, Rob, and I set out from Base Camp with twenty-pound packs and twice as much weight in our sleds. We skied the five and a half miles to Low Camp, situated on a flat expanse of glacier, away from any falling debris from the flanks. We ate dinner and drank tea until it was time to go to bed. The following morning we packed our fifty-pound packs, put on our crampons, and walked the quarter mile to the headwall, the steepest and most heavily crevassed section of our route. Although it is usual to cover terrain like this alone with a client, it was nice to have the added safety of a second guide on the rope. Within five hours of leaving Low Camp, we were greeted by the sight of High Camp, at just over twelve thousand feet. We would be staying here for a full day to acclimatize and rest for summit day, when we would be climbing nearly four thousand feet to the summit, then descending the same way back to High Camp. It was a big day for everyone, but especially for some of the clients who weren't accustomed to such extreme exertion in the mountains.

The thermometer in our tent registered minus thirty the entire time we were there. Rob and I stayed in one tent, while Heather stayed in her own just feet away. With the winds raging you couldn't hear anything between tents most of the time. I cooked hot food all day for Rob and myself, mainly soups, ramen, and the dehydrated dinners that were standard fare on the mountain. We were happy to have round-the-clock sunlight, which is the Antarctic summer's best feature.

We got up at seven the morning of our summit bid and were dressed and ready to go by 8:30. I was in my standard climbing clothes: long underwear, soft-shell pants, and a down sweater covered with a windproof jacket. We left the camp and climbed south toward a ridge, beyond which lay the top summit valley of Vinson. Twenty minutes later, as we crested the rim of this ridge, the full force of the wind hit me. Although I didn't have my thermometer on me, it felt like the temperature had dropped twenty degrees. We stopped to put on our down parkas and insulated pants, and I put my goggles on over my face mask and took out my high-altitude mittens.

We continued up the plateau, which was completely wind-scoured and bereft of signs that anyone had passed through in the previous two months.

The cold was piercing. I felt in no danger of freezing, but neither did I feel warm. Once we had crossed the plateau we gained the ridge proper, which would lead us upward to the summit. We were more exposed here and had to be mindful of where we placed our feet, and of any gusts that might knock us off balance. Because the temperatures were so cold and the howling wind prevented any but the most necessary dialogue, we were all in our own worlds as we moved along the ridge.

In the decades I had spent in the mountains, I had always enjoyed the adversity of inclement weather. I loved the challenge of putting myself out there and figuring out how to manage. I was in a state that I had grown to love: I felt light and empty, and the only thing I had to do was put one foot in front of the other and keep moving uphill toward my goal.

I began to think about all my years of therapy, and how climbing had been the best therapy of all. Far from the confusion of human civilization and interaction, I had found the simplicity and beauty I had longed for in my youth. On the flanks of mountains and in the challenge of scaling frozen waterfalls, I had come to know who I really was and what really mattered to me. I had observed the change as my mind, once riddled with confusing emotions and unbridled passions, learned how to hold a focus on a goal of my choosing. I also came to realize the power inherent in my being, and that a directed will could take me to heights I had once believed were reserved only for the select few.

But most of all I had learned to live not with fear and trepidation, but with a yearning to embrace what it meant to be human. In my years of searching I had arrived at my own philosophy of life, the essence of which was that existence is a precious gift, and that every moment, whether in the throes of joy or the pit of despair, is equally to be treasured.

As I reached the top, with terrain dropping away on all sides, an infinite view opened up before me. Standing on the roof of the wildest place on earth, my heart filled with emotion. My mind flashed back to the turning point in my life—sitting in a jail cell with concrete walls closing in on all sides—and I noted the stark contrast to where I was now. I thought of a line I had read long ago that gave me something to measure my progress by: It's not where you are that matters, but how far you've come.

EPILOGUE

ARCTIC DREAM

Four months after I stood on the summit of Mount Vinson, Karen and her climbing partner Sue Nott disappeared without a trace on the Infinite Spur, a remote alpine route in the Alaska Range. I was overcome with grief when I heard that my friend of twelve years had died, and I decided that the best homage I could pay Karen was to make her proud of the way I lived each of my remaining days.

A few months later I got a call from Kim Reynolds, the owner and founder of Chicks with Picks, a Colorado-based company that hosts clinics in which women learn to ice climb. She asked if I would be one of her guides for the upcoming season, filling the vacant spot created by Karen's death. I told her I would, and in January 2007 I drove to Ouray to instruct these clinics. I quickly realized that I got as much out of them as the women I taught. I loved nothing more than to share with them the activity that had literally changed my life. But there was an even more amazing gift I received from Chicks.

Shortly before I was busted in Jasper in 1992, I was leafing through a climbing magazine when I came upon the photo of a woman climbing up a crack in a rock face. I looked down at the caption and read her name: Kitty Calhoun. The image captured my attention, and this woman had become a role model for me. Now I discovered that one of my fellow Chicks with Picks guides was the very woman I had chosen as my inspiration fifteen years before.

While writing this book, I was often struck by the feeling that the life described in these pages could not possibly have been mine, so far removed do I feel from many of the activities and states of mind portrayed here. At the same time, it feels like everyone's story: any one of us could have made a string of bad choices, or lived through such dark experiences, ending up in a place we would rather not be.

I did not write my story because I thought it was different or remarkable. On the contrary, once I resurfaced into the world of the living, I saw parts of my story reflected everywhere around me: in the epidemic of depression sweeping North America, in the rampant sense of alienation in our culture, and in the skyrocketing statistics of addiction. I reconnected with my culture through these common themes, and I realized that while I may have been an extreme example, I am by no means alone. I began to feel that the greatest benefit of my experience would be for my story to help others.

If you were to ask me what got me through the pain and torment of my decades of depression, my answer would be hope. I always believed there was light at the end of the tunnel, even when I could see nothing but darkness. My angry, stubborn, and rebellious spirit refused to give in, no matter how painful life became, and for this I am eternally grateful.

I also refused to make excuses for myself, because at a certain point I realized that my salvation was mine alone to achieve. There were people and activities that could help me, but ultimately I knew I was responsible for the success of my healing. If I were asked to make a list of the things that helped me most, they would be talk therapy, exercise, diet, great friends, meditation, time spent in nature, and tanning salons during the darkest months.

People who are predisposed to drug addiction often have low levels of serotonin and dopamine. In his book *In the Realm of Hungry Ghosts*, Gabor Maté takes this a step further and makes the connection between low levels of serotonin and dopamine in the brain and childhood neglect and/or abuse. You may not find such a connection made in the mainstream media, but that should be a warning sign to those in search of truth. One of the saving graces of my healing is the fact that I trusted my own experience over what experts and authorities were saying. Had I listened to these people, I would probably be in a situation quite different from the one I find myself in today.

If you asked me to sum up the path I have taken in my life, I would put it this way: I have tried to make choices that would lead me to personal empowerment, that would lead me to become conscious of who I am and what I want to accomplish in my life. I have learned that happiness is an inside job. By taking the reins of one's life, one can overcome seemingly insurmountable odds. I have learned that the only thing required to live a healthy, stable life is the opportunity to make one healthy, stable choice after another. In this respect, life is no different than climbing a mountain or scaling a frozen waterfall. The final frontier for humankind is inner space, and I am climbing the mountains of my heart as well as those of the planet.

I have spent a great deal of my life trying to understand human behaviour, and I have asked myself repeatedly: Are humans inherently good, or evil? I have come to the conclusion that humans contain every possibility, and that what distinguishes them from each other is their choices. The only difference between the sinner and the saint, the cop and the criminal, the drug addict and the athlete is the choices they make when faced with their particular life circumstances.

The experiences of my life have taught me to be grateful—for everything, but especially for the simple things. There are people in the world who need healing, but who have not been as fortunate as I have been, or have not had the opportunities that I had. Thinking about them, no matter what their state of affairs, I think of the phrase that others may at one time have applied so aptly to me: *There, but for the grace of God, go I.*

In the summer of 2007 I was on a cruise ship anchored in Resolute Bay. My fellow crew members were using Zodiacs to take luggage to shore, and I was on the back deck savouring one last look at the vast and barren landscape of Canada's North. I heard footsteps and turned to see a well-dressed older woman walking toward me.

"I was very impressed with the presentation you gave on your wilderness adventures last night," she began. "I don't feel like I had as many lifestyle choices as you did when I was younger. But," she continued, "if I had the chance to go back and make different choices, I would do what you're doing. You are living my dream life."

AFTERWORD TO THE NEW EDITION

Throughout most of the story you've just read, I felt incredibly alone. Like there was no one else like me in the world. Like there was something wrong with me. But when I resurfaced from my journey into the depths of darkness and into the light of day, I saw shards of my story reflected everywhere around me: in the epidemic of depression sweeping North America, in the skyrocketing statistics of the opioid crisis, and in the rampant sense of alienation in our culture. I began to reconnect with others through these common themes, and I realized that while I may have been an extreme example, I am by no means alone.

What I didn't realize is that the events of my early life, rooted in intergenerational trauma, were but an offshoot of a society-wide dysfunction born from an invisible architecture of power that underlies all animal behaviour. It is the dark side of humanity—evil, if you will—and it is responsible for a system of power that hurts us all, but in particular, the most vulnerable and marginalized members of the tribe.

It is also destroying Nature at an unprecedented and alarming rate, so much so that the refuge I sought in the arms of the earth may not be available to a little Margo of the future. There is no singular problem that is at the root of this destruction, but rather, a toxic cultural soup reflected as a consciousness level that has forgotten that underneath all of the apparent variety and vicissitudes of the world, we are all connected, and our fates intertwined.

What drew me to ice climbing in the first place was the sheer immediacy of it. I had discovered an arena that had swift and decisive repercussions for my actions, for better or for worse. This arena was the antithesis of the world I grew up in, a world permeated by a powerful invisible undercurrent that ran through every interaction, every experience, and every relationship. And because it was invisible, it remained unnamed, wreaked its destruction silently, while its very existence was denied and unaccounted for. At the individual level, this invisible abuse of power is the root cause of what we term mental illness. At the cultural level, it underpins the mass psychology that allowed for the rise of Hitler, the invasion of Iraq, and the plethora of random shootings that plague us on an ever-increasing level.

Humanity is on the cusp of the most important leap in its evolution, and what will take us to the next level is nothing short of a shift in consciousness. We need to become an empowered species, and live up to our potential as intelligent, sensitive stewards of each other and of the planet. In order to do this, we need to face the role that trauma plays in the powerlessness that leads to tyranny. In other words, trauma doesn't come out of nowhere, and it doesn't go away. Collective trauma and the toxic culture it engenders is at the heart of human evil, and no amount of good will and positive thinking can alter this foundational underpinning of human existence. Only positive action can save us now. The good and the bad news is: it starts and ends with you...